MICHAEL L. JONES

Louisville
JUG MUSIC

From Earl McDonald to the
National Jubilee

THE
History
PRESS

Published by The History Press
Charleston, SC 29403
www.historypress.net

Copyright © 2014 by Michael L. Jones
All rights reserved

First published 2014

Manufactured in the United States

ISBN 978.1.62619.496.0

Library of Congress CIP data applied for.

This book is dedicated to Rod Wenz and Steve Drury, founders of the National Jug Band Jubilee. The two of them did so much to preserve the legacy of jug band music in Louisville, Kentucky. Say hello to Earl, fellows.

Tributes to National Jug Band Jubilee founders Rod Wenz and Steve "the Amazing Mr. Gil Fish" Drury at the 2010 Jubilee. Drury was also a member of the Juggernaut Jug Band. Wenz was a retired public relations executive who collected vintage folk and early jazz records. *Photo by Brian Bohannon, courtesy of the National Jug Band Jubilee.*

Contents

Preface

The book you are holding is the end result of two decades of odd coincidences. The first occurred in 1993, a couple of years after I moved back to Louisville after attending the University of Kentucky in Lexington. I was thumbing through import blues records at a store called Underground Sounds when I came across a record called *Clifford Hayes and the Jug Bands of Louisville*. It was from RST, an Austrian label, but I wondered if the title was referring to Louisville, Kentucky. After purchasing the record, I took it home and discovered that not only was it *my* Louisville, but also the liner notes were written by a lady named Brenda Bogert, who lived only a few blocks away.

The Bogerts' phone was answered by Brenda's husband, Pen, a historian at the Filson Historical Society. He was a little surprised that I'd gone to the trouble of seeking him out, but he dutifully filled me in on the basic history of jug band music in Louisville. What excited me most was that this is an aspect of the blues I hadn't heard about before. I was raised by my grandparents in a house that was full of blues and jazz, so when I went off to the University of Kentucky, I drifted toward more abrasive sounds like hip-hop and punk rock. But in 1991, I moved back to Louisville and was living with some high school friends who had a college rock band called Rabbit Manor. One day, our friend Chris Blaise left a compilation of Robert Johnson recordings at our house that made me listen to the music of my youth in a new way. I became obsessed with reading and listening to everything to do with the blues. But as a writer, I felt like I didn't really have much to add in writing about the genre. There were no famous bluesmen from Louisville, and at

Author Michael L. Jones with jugs from the J.C. Barnett collection at the Oldham County Historical Society. Barnett donated more than four hundred jugs to the historical society. Whiskey jugs were used in the nineteenth century to advertise drinking establishments. *Photo by Brian Bohannon.*

the time, I didn't know that the town had been a popular stop for traveling musicians. Bogert gave me the feeling there was still something to know about the blues.

Our conversation led me to seek out the Juggernaut Jug Band, the last remaining jug band in Louisville. I went to leader Steve Drury's house one afternoon to go through his archives. This led to a 1998 *Louisville Magazine* article about the group. It took a few years and another coincidence before I got around to writing about jug band music again. One of my early assignments for the *Louisville Eccentric Observer* (*LEO*), a local alternative weekly where I've worked for two decades, was to write about a new video store opening in the Highlands neighborhood in Louisville called Wild & Woolly Video. The owner, Todd Brashear, had been the bassist for an indie rock band called Slint when he was a teenager. Years after the band broke up, one of its songs was used in the soundtrack of a Larry Clark movie called *Kids*. The exposure led indie rock fans to rediscover Slint, and the band members, all college age now, started getting royalties. Brashear used his money to open the business.

Todd turned out to be not only a good interview subject but also a great guy. I became a regular customer, and one day, as we were talking about music, I mentioned something about jug band music. Not only did Todd know about it, but also, when he was on tour in England, he'd come across a blues magazine called *Storyville* that had a history of Louisville jug band music in it. If I was interested, Todd knew someone who had some back issues, and he could get them for me. I later found all the articles at my local library, but I would never have known they existed without Todd.

All the *Storyville* articles about jug band music were based on an unpublished manuscript by Fred Cox, an Indianapolis attorney who had done jug band research in the 1960s and '70s. Cox and his fellow researchers, John Harris and John Randolph, had actually been able to interview the jug band musicians. With Todd's help, I was able to cobble together everything that had been published from Cox's manuscript. It became the basis for a 2000 *LEO* article I wrote called "That Crazy Jug Band Sound." That article is still available on the Juggernaut Jug Band's website, www.juggernautjugband.com.

The Cox manuscript mentioned a record collector named Everett Mock, who remembered jug bands playing at his father's store in Southern Indiana when he was a kid. Unfortunately, Mock was dead by the time I found out about him, but Todd and I went to the New Albany home of his brother, Larry Mock. Larry also remembered seeing the Ballard Chefs at an in-store performance when he was a child, but he didn't have much else to offer. His brother's music collection had been donated to Indiana University, where it was sitting in storage. He was angry about that because his brother wanted the collection made available to the public. Everett Mock's papers would eventually be purchased by the Filson Historical Society, but they did not include the article about early jazz in Louisville that Cox mentions in his manuscript.

It was a few years after that article when jug music came up again. In 2003, I left Louisville for a few months to go to Chicago for a magazine writing fellowship at Northwestern University. When I came back, I was unemployed and looking for something to do. Reverend Louis Coleman, a Louisville civil rights leader, contacted me about helping him write his autobiography. Coleman and I would meet at a coffeehouse a couple of times a week to do interviews. One day, we were talking about other activists he'd been affiliated with over the years. These were people whom he called his soldiers. One of them was Mattie Mathis. Just as an aside, Coleman mentioned that Mathis's father had been a big blues musician. Still interested in blues, I asked him her father's name. Coleman couldn't remember, but he said he used to blow into a jug. It had turned out that I'd known Earl McDonald's daughter for years without even knowing it.

Unfortunately, Mattie was in a nursing home by the time I found out she was related to Earl. I went to see her, thinking it might make for a good story, but she was suffering from a form of Alzheimer's disease, and her memory was better on some days than others. At the same time, I was working on a compilation of my writing called *Second-Hand Stories: 15 Portraits of Louisville*. When the book came out, I included the jug band article. Unbeknownst to me, Rod Wenz had started the National Jug Band Jubilee in 2005 to celebrate the legacy of jug band music in Louisville. The first Jubilee was a cruise on the *Belle of Louisville* that cost fifty dollars, way out of the price range of a struggling writer. However, in 2008, the festival was held in Waterfront Park for free. Rod invited me to sell my book there. This began a long association between Rod and me, and in conjunction, the Jubilee and me.

Rod and I hit it off instantly because, prior to being a public relations executive, he had been a journalist. He actually lived not far from me in the Highlands, and we'd meet occasionally and listen to music. Rod had already been doing jug band research for a while, so we got together to compare notes. It was Rod who first had the idea of doing a history of Louisville jug music, and he suggested that I be the one to write it. He offered to help me do the research, but Rod felt that I could bring a unique perspective to the music and Louisville culture being an African American. One of the ongoing problems of the National Jug Band Jubilee was that not many African Americans were attracted to the festival each year. Rod felt a book by an African American would help others to embrace the music. I agreed, and we had just started working together when Rod died in November 2008. Drury said he'd help me when he could after that, but he, too, died in November 2009. That left me the last man standing.

When I tell people that I write about jug band music, they usually ask why. They don't understand why an African American man would be so interested in the genre. That's because the most common image of a jug band is a hillbilly group at a square dance. After I explain that the first jug bands were African American and that jug blowing itself has precedents in Africa, they are a little more understanding. The main purpose of this book is to liberate jug music from the misconceptions that surround it. But I also hope that it provides a context for a general audience to appreciate the music, whether it is made by white or black artists. Jug band music played an important role in the development of a lot of music that people listen to today. Sometimes I joke that the history of jug music is like the secret history of rock-and-roll, but I'm only half joking.

Researching the life of Earl McDonald, and the lives of the various jug band musicians who worked with him, has given me a new perspective on the city I live in and my place in it. I realized that I'd been surrounded by the ghosts of these men for years without even knowing it. McDonald is buried in Louisville Cemetery, the oldest black cemetery in the city. It is less than two miles from the house I grew up in. The majority of Louisville's African American community lives on the west side of the city, so during my research, I often came across landmarks I knew or addresses that were familiar to me.

After Rod died, I took his place on the National Jug Band Jubilee Board of Directors. This brought me in contact with many traveling musicians, who offered me some insight into the genre. The last coincidence I experienced occurred a few years ago in the University of Louisville Library. I decided to see what the library had on jug music. The librarian brought me a file with two things in it: a copy of my jug band article and a page of handwritten notes from Fred Cox about mentions of Earl McDonald in the *Louisville Leader*, an early black newspaper. I felt like Cox was communicating with me from the dead.

There are many other people who contributed to the creation of this book. Chief among them are Heather Leoncini and the board of directors of the National Jug Band Jubilee, especially Gloria Wenz, Valerie Metry, David Wood, Aaron Coffey, Myron Koch and the late Tom Peterson. Special recognition should go to Gloria for giving me access to Rod's files. I would also like to thank the staff at the Filson Historical Society, Keith Clements and the Kentuckiana Blues Society, Terri Brown (Earl McDonald's granddaughter) and the late Ola Thornton (Sara Martin's adopted daughter) for their assistance. I have to acknowledge my wife, Melissa Amos-Jones, for being so patient with me; the University of Louisville Photo Archives; Dr. Abdul Buridi and the staff at DaVita Broadway (Diane, Linda, Sharon and Karen) for keeping me fit; and former *Highlander Neighborhood Monthly* publisher/editor Mary Jean Kirtley and photographer Brian Bohannon for their unending support of this project.

Introduction

Derby City Blues

Country music scholars have long acknowledged the significance of African American influences on country music prior to World War II in the form of ragtime and blues, vocal and instrumental styles, musical mentors and even the West African–derived banjo. But they have far less often recognized the actual participation of African Americans in the recording of this music, then called "hillbilly music" or, alternatively, "old-time music."
—*Patrick Huber,* Black Hillbillies: African American Musicians on Old-Time Records, 1924–1932

When most people think of a jug band, they picture a group of hillbillies like the Darlings from *The Andy Griffith Show* or the Muppets from Jim Henson's *Emmet Otter's Jug Band Christmas*. That's because jug band music is usually depicted as something rural and unrefined. But actually, the opposite is true. Jug music is a relatively modern and sophisticated sound that played a significant role in the development of contemporary American popular culture. It is part of a string band tradition that lies at the roots of blues, jazz, ragtime, bluegrass and country music. Yes, hillbillies played the jug, but so did southern slaves, riverboat roustabouts, blackface minstrels, medicine show peddlers and songsters working street corners in major urban centers. Until recently, both the origins and pervasive practice of jug blowing have been obscured by popular myth and societal prejudice.

Jug band music is often called mountain music because it is identified with the Appalachian Mountains, where jug blowing was a common practice. But

The Ballard Chefs at an in-store performance. The Ballard & Ballard Flour Company sponsored the group. It also had a popular radio show on WHAS in Louisville. *Courtesy of the University of Louisville Photographic Archives & Special Collections.*

the tradition came from Africa with the slaves and spread to whites as they adopted the African banjo. These musicians used homemade instruments to create the first original American music by combining African rhythms with European melodies. These old-time tunes were spread across the country by white minstrels, who sought to imitate and mock southern slaves. After the Civil War, black and white songsters also drew from this tradition in towns along the Ohio and Mississippi Rivers.

Jug music is not a monolithic sound. The groups have some regional characteristics. Memphis bands, being close to the Mississippi Delta, developed a sound akin to the country blues. Louisville jug bands were influenced by the New Orleans jazz arriving by riverboat at the Louisville Wharf. These were not your average street groups. They included jazz instrumentation like the saxophone, clarinet and piano, along with the usual string band instruments and the jug. For this reason, Louisville jug music stands out as unique. Major groups like the Dixieland Jug Blowers and Earl McDonald's Original Louisville Jug Band are usually classified as proto-jazz rather than folk or blues.

Louisville is considered the home of jug music because it produced the first jug band to record in the studio. In September 1924, four members of the Louisville Jug Band went into the studio with singer Sara Martin, the highest-paid black vaudeville entertainer of her time. Born in Louisville in 1884, Martin was already middle aged when she signed her first recording deal with the Okeh label in 1922.

The blues is usually associated with male troubadours straight from the Mississippi cotton fields with guitars and hard-luck stories. However, the first blues singers to record were actually glamorous, vaudeville-trained women like Martin. In 1920, Mamie Smith, an African American singer from Cincinnati, had a million-selling hit called "Crazy Blues." The song was written by Perry Bradford and produced by Ralph S. Peer for Okeh Records. The success of "Crazy Blues" ignited an interest in "race records," recordings by African American artists. Every label wanted to capitalize on the hit by signing its own roster of classic blues singers. Martin was among the earliest of them. She had a string of hits with New Orleans composer and bandleader Clarence Williams for Okeh and the Victor Talking Machine Company, where Peer moved in the mid-1920s.

In addition to singing, Martin was something of a talent scout for Peer. She introduced him to Louisville guitarist Sylvester Weaver, whose record "Guitar Rag" was the first to feature a slide guitar. Victor was attempting to cash in on a craze for novelty instruments when the company sent Martin into the studio with four members of the Louisville Jug Band: Earl McDonald, jug; Clifford Hayes, violin; Curtis Hayes, guitar; and Cal Smith, banjo.

The ten sides produced at these sessions were released in 1925, credited to Sara Martin's Jug Band. These were the first of a string of recordings that would ignite a national jug band craze that would exhaust itself only during the Great Depression. The nexus of musicians who made up the Louisville Jug Band would record for different labels under several different names—the Dixieland Jug Blowers, the Old Southern Jug Band, Earl McDonald's Original Louisville Jug Band and the Louisville Stompers being chief among them. The constants in all these groups were Earl McDonald and Clifford Hayes, whose collaboration is the heart of Louisville jug music. American music historian Samuel Charters also admired the pair's mixture of the rural black string band tradition and urban ragtime. In the liner notes to a Smithsonian Folkways jug band compilation, Charters wrote:

> *The Dixieland Jug Blowers were the greatest of the city jug bands, and in their music can be heard a brilliant fusion of the rough country jug with the most highly developed jazz of the middle twenties. The band was able to move from one mood to another without hesitation, and their recordings are of a high level of excellence.* Florida Blues *is remarkable for the fine jug solos of Earl McDonald, who is perhaps the finest jug player ever to record, and on* Banjoreno, *a tour-de-force for tenor, plectrum, and six string banjos, it is Cal Smith who drives the band.*

Earl McDonald is one of the most celebrated jug players in Louisville history. He was born in South Carolina on October 2, 1885, but his family moved to Kentucky when he was a toddler. Inspired by early street bands, he founded the Louisville Jug Band in 1902. The group started out on the street like other jug bands but was soon performing at house parties for the city's elite. In 1903, the Louisville Jug Band became the first jug band to perform at Churchill Downs on Kentucky Derby Day. In 1915, the group signed a deal with the Old Grand-Dad Distillery in Hobbs, Kentucky, to perform as the Old Grand-Dad Jug Band.

McDonald's main collaborator was Clifford Hayes, a fiddler who was born in Glasgow, Kentucky, in 1893. Hayes came from a musical family, which included banjo and guitar virtuoso Cal Smith, his nephew. Hayes moved to Louisville around 1912 and played in several string bands before joining the Louisville Jug Band in 1914.

A historical plaque at Waterfront Park in Louisville, Kentucky, honoring jug blower Earl McDonald. The National Jug Band Jubilee is held at Waterfront Park on the third Saturday in September of each year. *Photo by Brian Bohannon, courtesy of the National Jug Band Jubilee.*

The Louisville jug band musicians were quite versatile. Working together for more than a decade, Hayes and McDonald recorded with artists as diverse as country legend Jimmie Rodgers ("Good Girl Gone Blues") and jazz great Johnny Dodds ("House Rent Rag"). However, the Hayes-McDonald partnership was frayed by disputes over credit and money. Hayes made several attempts to play straightforward jazz without the jug, but he was forced to add it back to his group after McDonald's success with another Louisville band, the Ballard Chefs. Sponsored by Ballard & Ballard Flour Company, the Ballard Chefs had their own radio show in Louisville, and the group toured widely throughout the Southwest.

The appeal of jug band music began to wane during the Great Depression. Although they generated some interest during the American folk revival in the 1960s, Louisville jug band musicians have largely been forgotten except among early blues aficionados who continue to listen to the old 78s. One reason for their obscurity is that they do not fit into the accepted narrative of American popular music. In the early days of the recording industry, record companies advertised music of southern white artists as "hillbilly music," and black artists were classified under "race records." This segregated marketing was usually the rule, even when they were recording similar material or participating in interracial recording sessions.

The Louisville jug bands have the misfortune of being too hillbilly for most blues and jazz researchers and too urban for country music or bluegrass historians. In fact, the whole African American string band tradition has basically been ignored, as has the role of black vaudeville artists like Martin in shaping black popular music. Certain regions have become identified and limited to certain styles of music: blues in the Mississippi, jazz in New Orleans and country music in the Appalachian Mountains. But Louisville jug band music drew on elements of them all.

Another reason that Louisville jug music has not received the attention it deserves is that there are aspects of the genre that can make some people uncomfortable. Many of the jug band songs were first transmitted through blackface minstrel shows. Some of them are rife with racial stereotypes. However, when they are viewed in the context of their time, these tunes have a different story to tell.

The minstrel show was the most popular form of entertainment in the United States for almost a half century, and it continues to have an undeniable influence on contemporary American culture. This was the arena in which black performers worked, but they were able to play with and ridicule some of the popular stereotypes around them. Some of the more outwardly offensive jug band songs take on slightly different meanings in the hands of black performers. For example, the Earl McDonald's Original Louisville Jug Band recorded an Irving Jones composition called "Under the Chicken Tree" that typifies what were known as "coon songs." The song features McDonald singing about a dream where chickens and hens grow on trees. While the subject matter fits in the minstrel tradition, McDonald clearly views it as satire and not a real interpretation of black life. He plies every line with bits of comedy.

"A lot of the history around the Louisville jug bands has not been written down in a way that is easy for people to digest," said Dom Flemons, a founding member of the Carolina Chocolate Drops, a contemporary African American string band. "It's black minstrel music, but it's black-run and black-owned minstrel music, if that makes sense. When you hear 'Under the Chicken Tree,' yes it is racist. But what an amazing composition they are presenting. Even the sketches in the middle of it, you can hear that it is black humor on top of the stereotypes invented by white people doing blackface."

McDonald and his generation of jug musicians were children of the Jazz Age. They translated a nineteenth-century tradition for a country thrown into modernity by World War I. Jug band music is sometimes called happy or good-time music because it is meant for parties and frolic in the Jazz Age. McDonald and his compatriots made records full of humor and amazing musicianship. If nothing else, they deserve to be the people we think of when we speak about jug band musicians.

Chapter 1
The Roots of Jug Music

[The] *music* [that] *formed the link between pure African music and the music*
[that] *developed after the African slave in the United States had a chance*
to become exposed to some degree of Euro-American culture was that which
contained the greatest number of Africanisms and yet was foreign to Africa.
—*LeRoi Jones,* Blues People: Negro Music in White America

Bill Livers was born on August 3, 1911, in Owenton, Kentucky, about sixty miles from Louisville. His parents were tenant farmers, and Livers spent most of his life following the same occupation. He credited farming with getting him through the Great Depression. Livers was also a fiddler who earned extra money by performing with string bands in the region. Occasionally, one of his bands would use a jug player. "He was the real deal," says John Harrod, who documented traditional fiddle styles in Kentucky. "He came from a family of black musicians around New Liberty, and he was my first direct contact with a real traditional musician in Kentucky."

Livers started playing the fiddle in 1937 after he bought a two-hundred-year-old instrument that was strung for a left-handed player. After he had the fiddle restrung for a right-handed player, Livers said it took a year for him to learn how to play the thing again. Livers's bands played traditional fiddle tunes like "Down Yonder" and "Up and Down Eagle Creek," standards in his part of Kentucky. They also played some blues. In an interview published in *Living Blues* magazine in 1981, Livers revealed that he learned to play the blues from a man who came to town with a carnival. This wasn't another

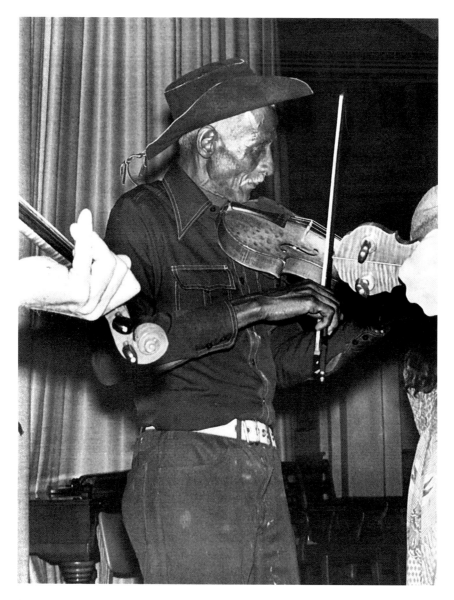

Old-time fiddler Bill Livers. Livers played in a string band in Owenton, Kentucky. *Courtesy of Berea College Special Collections & Archives.*

fiddler; rather, the man played a comb. Livers remembered that he "sang the blues, then he'd get to it and blow that comb and just moan; you'd think he was a million miles away. He came here with the carnival, and he didn't stay here about three days."

Kazoos! The modern kazoo was modeled after a traditional African horn. *Photo by Brian Bohannon, courtesy of National Jug Band Jubilee.*

To play the comb, a person places a piece of paper over the teeth and blows into it. The sound is similar to a kazoo. The concept is the same. They are both membranophones, instruments that depend on a vibrating membrane to make sound. The kazoo is a plastic or metal tube with two open ends, one flattened and the other circular. There is a third opening a little off center in the tube, nearer the flattened end, that leads to a small chamber housing a wax membrane. It is played by a person humming or speaking into it. The modern kazoo is based on an 1840 design by Alabama Vest, an African American man from Macon, Georgia, and first manufactured by a German-born clockmaker named Thaddeus Von Glegg. But Vest's creation was based on African horns called mirilons. These membranophones have a long and surprising history.

Archaeologist Henry Balfour, the first curator of the Pitts River Museum at Oxford University, published a number of papers that used artifacts as a jumping-off point for an examination of human evolution. He wrote an influential article about the musical bow, which he considered the forefather of all stringed instruments. Balfour discovered that some cultures in West Africa and India used membranophones to represent the voice of spirits in ritual ceremonies or to disguise their own voices from them during these rituals. He was working on a paper on the subject when he died in 1939. In "Ritual and Secular Uses of Vibrating Membranes as Voice Disguisers,"

Spoons ready for the workshop. Some of the early jug bands featured spoon players. *Photo by Brian Bohannon, courtesy of National Jug Band Jubilee.*

which was completed by his friends after he passed away, Balfour described a ceremony he witnessed in an Ibo village in Nigeria.

Balfour saw two men, representing dead spirits, wearing masks and rags to conceal their identities. Each man held a small reed tube in his mouth. One end of the tube was open, and the other was covered by a thin white membrane believed to be a spider egg cyst. Balfour observed that "when they spoke or sang, the membranes were thrown into vibration, causing the voices to sound harsh and nasal, a quality associated with spirit voices." Elsewhere in the paper, Balfour also described the reaction of another observer who thought the horns sounded "very like that made by blowing through a comb enveloped in thin paper."

These voice disguisers were the ancestors of the modern kazoo, which happens to be a popular jug band instrument. Balfour found that at some point in time, these voice disguisers lost their ritual use and were eventually used as children's instruments in some parts of the world. He also thought that a European novelty instrument, the Eunuch's Horn, might have once served a ritual purpose. This led him to conclude that "the playthings of advanced cultures frequently have an interesting and suggestive past history, traceable back to times when their prototypes functioned in all seriousness and when they even played a part as accessories in ritual. Their ritualistic use, indeed, has frequently caused them to be overlooked by investigators who have not been privileged to penetrate 'behind the scenes' of native ceremonial."

When Europeans began importing Africans to the New World, they considered their new bondsmen to be blank vessels without culture. However, the Africans

descended from cultures in modern-day Angola, Nigeria and the Congo with long traditions of transmitting family lore, tribal history and other useful information through song, dance and folktales. This oral tradition, especially as it involved music, survived among the descendants of enslaved Africans as what Melville Herskovits called "Africanisms." That is not to say that these traditions remained static throughout the years. As subsequent generations were born into slavery in the United States, they adapted African models and melodies, along with European influences, into a number of new musical hybrids. Blues, jazz and gospel music all evolved concurrently from the Negro spirituals and work songs that form the basis of African American culture. So did jug band music.

When the African contribution to American music is discussed, most of the conversation usually centers on call and response, polyrhythms and the functionality of music. But an Africanism that receives little recognition is the ingenuity to make something from nothing. Where the drum or other traditional musical instruments were not available, slaves made music with whatever was at hand. The Federal Writers' Project of the Works Progress Administration's Slave Narratives are full of stories about slaves turning household items into musical instruments. Wash Wilson, a former Louisiana slave, remembered:

> Dere wasn't no music instruments. Us take pieces of a sheep's rib or cow's jaw or a piece of iron, with a old kettle, or a hollow gourd and some horse hair to make the drum…Dey'd take de buffalo horn and scrape it out to make de flute. Dat sho' be heard a long ways off. Then dey'd take a mule's jaw-bone, and rattle de stick 'cross its teeth.

In her study of early African American music, *Sinful Tunes and Spirituals: Black Folk Music to the Civil War*, Dena J. Epstein found that southern slaves were making music with household items like washboards and stonemason jars by the beginning of the nineteenth century. There is a direct African precedent for this. Among the Bantu people of Central Africa, there is an instrument known as the chipeni, or singing gourd. A person plays the hollowed gourd by vocalizing into it much like a jug, which is not a coincidence. In *Deep Blues*, blues historian Robert Palmer says jug blowing is a direct descendant of gourd playing. Palmer reported:

> One fascinating group of instruments, singing horns and singing gourds, can be played as horns, with the lips vibrating, or simply used as megaphones to amplify the voice. The Luba of Zaire lip their singing gourds as if they are playing trumpets, and the instruments contribute propulsive bass parts to the ensemble music. The playing techniques, and the instrument's musical function, were preserved by the jug blowers in black American jug bands.

Ethnomusicologist Hugh Tracey spent some time with the chipeni-playing Luba and Lulua people of the Democratic Republic of Congo in the 1950s. His recordings are available on two Smithsonian Folkways albums, *Dances and Various Songs from the Luba of the Democratic Republic of Congo* and *Ceremonial, Topical, and Dance Songs from the Luba of the Democratic Republic of Congo*. The music includes chipeni players and people beating on bottles, among other instruments. *Dances and Various Songs* includes a truly amazing track called "Chitululedumulombashinka," which has male and female singers accompanied by a symphony of singing gourds. The rhythm is so dense and pronounced that it could be a track from a funk group like Parliament-Funkadelic or the Ohio Players. The song brings to mind something that Louisville jug player Rudolph "Jazz Lips" Thompson once told an interviewer, "A good jug player has to learn to play by ear and keep time. If he gets off the time, he throws the whole band off."

The link between Africa and the Louisville jug bands of the 1920s is old-time music, which has roots in Africa and Europe but is uniquely American. The story of this genre centers mainly on the fiddle and the banjo, although an old-time string band can include a number of other plucked instruments. The fiddle was a popular folk instrument throughout the British Isles that was introduced to Europe by the Byzantine Empire in the tenth century. The banjo came from Africa with the slaves. African banjos had bodies made from gourds, necks crafted from sticks and a varying number of strings. Thomas Jefferson, in his *Notes on the State of Virginia*, mentions the "banjar" as the main instrument of slaves.

The blues is often identified with the guitar, but the fiddle and banjo were actually the most common instruments for black musicians in the nineteenth century. This pairing is the most frequent combination in the traditional string band, where jug blowing prospered. In most cases, when we find jug blowing in America, it is used as accompaniment for either the banjo or fiddle as a rhythm instrument playing the bass lines.

The jug has been called the poor man's tuba, but jug blowing requires a different embouchure than a brass instrument. The jug blower holds the opening inches from their face and makes a buzzing sound into it. The container acts as a resonating chamber, amplifying the noise. Tone and pitch are controlled by loosening and tightening the lips and changing the angle of the jug. As an instrument, the jug has only a two-octave range, but a talented player can do a lot within that space.

Most contemporary people view the banjo, fiddle and jug blowing as merely components of bluegrass music, but that's because their use in other genres has been obscured by history. The fiddle was introduced to America by Europeans, mainly the Scots-Irish. The settlers from Lowland Scotland originally migrated to the farmlands of Ulster, Ireland, in the seventeenth century, but economic pressure from the English government soon pushed them to the New World. More than 150,000 Scots-Irish entered the United States before 1770. They brought with them not only the fiddle but also ballads and dances like reels and jigs.

The Scots-Irish settled in Appalachia and the Ohio Valley, where they became the dominant culture. This is why old-time music is sometimes referred to as mountain music. The earliest Scots-Irish settlers came to Kentucky through the

Cumberland Gap and on flatboats floating down the Ohio River. They had permanent settlements in the area by 1770. These settlers brought slaves with them to work the land. This resulted in the musical fusion that resulted in the Appalachian music styles.

A lot of space has been wasted trying to separate the European influences in American music from the African ones, but in actuality, there was a continuous dialogue, borrowing and synthesis among all cultures in the United States. The situation is made even more complex by the fact that Europe and Africa share some universal musical characteristics. In *Urban Blues*, Charles Keil pointed out that African and European music are "enough alike to blend easily in a seemly infinite array of hybrids." Keil also quoted Marshall Stearns's *The Story of Jazz*, which stated that "European folk music is a little more complicated harmonically and African tribal music is a little more complicated rhythmically. They are about equal in terms of melody…when the African arrived in the New World the folk music that greeted him must have sounded familiar enough, except for the lack of rhythm."

Old-time music was the result of the cultural interaction between slave and master. There was no general European or African musical style common to all the people who ended up in the United States. The Africans who were taken into bondage did not come from identical musical traditions, but their music shared some specific characteristics. The same is true of the European settlers. Old-time music represents the fusion of various regional European and African musical traditions.

The biggest distinction between the European settlers and their bondsmen was the way they thought of and used music. In Africa, art was functional. Bowls, dances and masks may have been beautiful, but they also served a purpose. The slaves, because their creative outlets were limited, depended on music, folktales and dance as their main cultural outlets. Furthermore, this was also in keeping with the African mindset because their oral traditions valued these particular arts. In Africa, the way a song was played often said as much to the audience as the words. Some deities had their own melodies, and drumming was used to communicate messages. In fact, this was the reason that South Carolina outlawed the drum in 1740 following the Stono Rebellion.

The Stono Rebellion began on a plantation near the Stono River in Charleston, South Carolina, when a group of slaves stole weapons and ammunition from a warehouse. They were reacting to a rumor that the Spanish had promised freedom to any African who made it to St. Augustine, Florida. The revolt leaders were joined by other slaves. Led by an Angolan slave, they marched to the beat of two drums and killed anyone who tried to stop them.

Adam Wirtzfeld of the Roe Family Singers teaching a saw workshop. His Kirkwood Hollow, Minnesota group blends characteristic old-time sound with rock-and-roll urgency and influence. *Photo by Brian Bohannon, courtesy of the National Jug Band Jubilee.*

The Stono Rebellion, and a few other uprisings that happened around the same time, led to new restrictions on the activity of slaves in South Carolina and other colonies. One of the prohibitions was the banning of the drum, but rhythm was such an important component of the slaves' concept of music that they internalized the instrument. Hand clapping, foot stomping and dancing evolved in a way that took the place of the drums. Percussion is an essential component in all African American music and dance. It has even influenced the way black musicians play Western instruments. Many of the bluegrass and country music legends from Kentucky have stories of learning music from African American musicians. Bluegrass pioneer Bill Monroe acknowledged the influence of Arnold Shultz, a black guitarist and fiddler. Western Kentucky became famous for a thumb-picking guitar style passed on from black musicians to white ones like Merle Travis and Chet Atkins.

"See, I was born in 1910, it was back there in about the time I was just a little boy," Bill Livers remembered in the interview. "There were musicians…you never heard such a playin'. Burn them strings up! Burn 'em up!"

Bill Livers was interviewed for *Living Blues* by Burnham Ware, grandnephew of Claud Livers, who played mandolin and guitar with him in a string band. By the beginning of the twentieth century, jug blowing was a common part of the string band combo in black and white bands in Kentucky. Livers remembered a man named Navy Pitts, who played jug and washboard for his group:

> *Navy Pitts run a shoe shop there. And the guy over at New Liberty—have you heard of Ches Morton? Chester Morton had a 12-string guitar, you see, they ain't got but six on them, but he had a double string steel guitar. Navy was on the washboard and Sylvester, he was on the drums and Chester, he was on that 12-string guitar. And they played up—oh, they drawed the awfulest crowd. They played up there in the courthouse yard. Play up there maybe once every two months…they played for all the tap dances and all the concerts, around here in New Liberty.*

This is the foundation on which Louisville jug music developed. The genre grew differently in Louisville than it did in other parts of the country for several reasons. The city is called the "Gateway to the South" because it sits on the border between the Midwest and the Deep South. Louisville jug band music reflects the influences of these two geographic extremes. These groups married the northern urge for newness and progress with traditional southern culture. Chief among the reason for this is the fact that the River City was a major nineteenth-century shipping port. It was a frequent destination for people working or doing business along the Ohio and Mississippi Rivers. This provided multiple opportunities for musical cross-pollination with New Orleans and other river ports. Louisville musicians incorporated jazz styles as they were being created. In fact, they probably contributed to the formation of some of them. Economic opportunity also attracted settlers—Scots-Irish, French and German—who contributed their own unique flavor to the city's culture.

The biggest contributor to Louisville jug band music was the city's African American population, which is drawn from all over the state. Louisville was a Union stronghold during the Civil War. Bondsmen migrated to the city in search of freedom during the war, and after emancipation, more freedmen poured into the city in search of family and work. To this day, the majority of African Americans in Kentucky reside within the boundaries of Louisville. This population left a legacy of folk and professional musicians that would produce the first generation of jug bands. The act of blowing into a bottle to create sound may go back to prehistoric times, but it became an art form in Louisville, Kentucky.

Chapter 2
The City by the Falls

The place that's right for that love sight is in those bluegrass hills
Where gently flows the Ohio by a place called Louisville.
—"Eight More Miles to Louisville," a song by Louis Marshall Jones,
aka Grandpa Jones

Louisville, Kentucky, exists because of the Falls of the Ohio, a series of rapids formed by the erosion of a limestone shelf where the Ohio River drops twenty-six feet over the length of two and a half miles. The Falls of the Ohio is the only natural impediment to river travel on the Ohio for the nearly one thousand miles between the waterway's origins in Pittsburgh, Pennsylvania, and Cairo, Illinois, where it feeds into the Mississippi River. Today, this obstacle is controlled by a series of locks and dams that are part of the Louisville and Portland Canal, which was first built in 1830. Before this, ships had to unload their cargo on one end of the Falls and carry it to the other end by land while a guide helped the vessel navigate the rocky rapids. It was impossible to cross the Falls of the Ohio during periods of low water.

Controlling the Falls was an important goal for both the British and the Continental armies during the American Revolution. In 1778, General George Rogers Clark founded the City by the Falls in order to use it as a base of operations against British forces in the West. Clark was born in Charlottesville, Virginia, on November 19, 1752, the second of ten children. One of his brothers was the explorer William Clark, a leader of the famous 1803 Lewis and Clark expedition that mapped out the West after the

LOU. RESTAURANT OPERATORS ASSN.
MEETING JAN., 31, 1939
COMPLIMENTS OF JOHN G. EPPING.

The Louisville Master Bakers Jug Band. The group is pictured in front of a crowd of restaurant association conference attendees. *Courtesy of the University of Louisville Photographic Archives & Special Collections.*

Louisiana Purchase. In fact, William Clark and his partner, Meriwether Lewis, started their trip in the Louisville area. Most of the members of their company were men recruited from Louisville and southern Indiana. Sculptor Ed Hamilton, creator of the black Civil War Memorial in Washington, D.C., also did a statue of Lewis and Clark's slave guide, York, which stands on the riverfront at Fifth and Main Streets in Louisville's downtown. William Clark's grandson, Colonel Meriwether Lewis Clark Jr., was instrumental in the founding of Churchill Downs and the running of the first Kentucky Derby in 1875.

George Rogers Clark is best remembered as a soldier, but he was working as a surveyor when he first visited Kentucky in 1772. The land that would become the Commonwealth of Kentucky was Native American hunting territory for centuries until Europeans started wandering into the area about 1750. George came with the wave of settlers who were setting down roots in what was then considered the West. But the permanent settlements did not sit well with the Native Americans. Hostilities with the tribes led the Kentucky settlers to seek protection from Virginia. George was one of two men charged with delivering a petition for help to the governor. The Virginia legislature created Kentucky County, Virginia, in 1776.

George made his name fighting against the Native American tribes as part of the Virginia militia, but he was on a mission from the Continental army when he founded Louisville. The British, who claimed Kentucky because of a treaty with the Iroquois, were arming the Native American tribes against the colonists. George Rogers Clark traveled with 150 volunteer soldiers, their families and possessions down the Ohio River on flatboats. The group landed on Corn Island, a small body of land that has since been reclaimed by the Ohio. By the time Christmas arrived, the settlers had built a fort on the mainland. That first Christmas in Kentucky is where the story of Louisville music begins.

The first musician in Louisville was a slave named Cato Watts. Not much is known about him except that he was a fiddler, and he was owned by a man named Captain John Donne. They were among the first settlers who landed on Corn Island. In fact, Watts's renown with his instrument has become an essential part of Louisville lore.

Watts often entertained the settlers with his fiddle during those early months of hard work, but as Christmas approached, he found himself with only one string on his instrument. Fortunately, a Frenchman named Jean Nickle arrived in the settlement before the holidays to have repairs done to his canoe. A fellow musician, Nickle traded Watts strings in exchange for coonskins. With his fiddle whole again, Watts expected to perform at the Christmas celebration. However, the settlers disappointed him by asking Nickle to provide the music instead. It did not go well. According to Reuben T. Durrett, author of 1880's *Romance of the Origin of Louisville*, Nickle's music was too European high culture for backwoods people who wanted to dance. Durrett related:

> On the 25th of December, 1778, they celebrated their first Christmas in the wilderness with a feast and a dance in this Twelfth Street fort. They called it a house-warming, and every man, woman, and child of the settlement took part in it. A Frenchman, who happened there at the time, attempted to supply the music for the dance, but he was too scientific and was soon supplanted by an old Negro named Cato Watts, whose fiddle gave them Virginia reels and Irish jigs, and such other lively tunes as they wanted.

There are other accounts explaining that the settlers asked Nickle to perform because Watts was lost in a storm. In these versions, Watts steps out of the forest and grabs the instrument from the Frenchman to the delight of the dancers. Incidentally, in addition to being the first musician in the city, Watts was also the first person to be executed in Louisville. He was hanged in 1787 after killing Donne in a hunting accident. His life illustrates the two extremes African Americans would endure in Louisville over the next two hundred years.

Louisville was an important trading post from its inception, and the city's influence grew even more after the steamboat was introduced to the Ohio and Mississippi Rivers. In fact, Louisville was one of the largest cities in the country during the nineteenth century. The city experienced explosive population growth almost from the beginning. Between 1790 and 1850, according to census records, Louisville's population grew from two hundred to just over forty thousand people. A major reason for the city's success was its proximity to the Ohio River. The large influx of people and wealth into Louisville was largely a result of an exciting new nineteenth-century technological innovation: the steam engine.

The first steamboat in the Louisville Harbor was the aptly named *New Orleans*, which made it possible for Louisville to trade with the boat's city. The *New Orleans* was partly owned by Robert Fulton and Robert Livingston, who constructed a one-paddle-wheel boat called the *Clermont* that ferried passengers between New York City and Albany in 1807. The pair joined forces with Nicholas Roosevelt, Theodore Roosevelt's great-grand-uncle,

A jug band at a Louisville Gas & Electric Company employee picnic. Companies often hired African American bands to entertain at gatherings. *Courtesy of the University of Louisville Photographic Archives & Special Collections.*

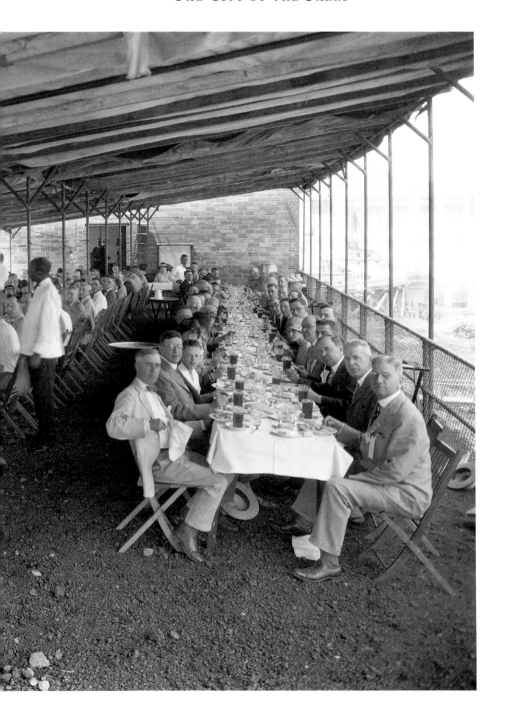

to create a vessel capable of opening up river commerce on the Ohio and Mississippi. In 1811, Roosevelt unveiled the fruits of their labor, the *New Orleans*, by taking a yearlong trip from Pittsburgh to the city of New Orleans.

When the *New Orleans* arrived in Louisville in October 1811, the Ohio River was so low that the ship was unable to cross the rocky terrain at the Falls of the Ohio. It was stuck in Louisville for weeks. The crew passed time by giving rides to locals. The ship also made a roundtrip to Cincinnati, something many people thought was impossible. Prior to steam power, human muscle had been the only way to get upstream; rowboats, poles or towlines were the only ways to move against the current. The *New Orleans* did about eight miles per hour downstream and three miles per hour against the upstream Ohio River current. The steamboats got even faster as the years progressed, which encouraged more river traffic and more commerce in Louisville. This transformed the city's culture. This riverboat traffic tied Louisville, commercially and culturally, to other river towns like St. Louis, Cincinnati and New Orleans. These cities came to mirror one another in many aspects, including the fact that all of them produced notable jug bands. String and brass bands appeared in Louisville at the same time as they did in New Orleans. Louisville jug band musicians like Clifford Hayes would develop close associations with musicians in Cincinnati and other river towns.

The city's influence grew even more after the Civil War, in large part because the Louisville & Nashville Railroad controlled a majority of the working railways to the South. Louisville's economic success attracted people from different origins. The Scots-Irish, German, French, ex-Confederates and African Americans all contributed to the city's music culture.

Many of the first black residents entered Kentucky in chains. The Commonwealth of Kentucky was a slave territory when it entered the Union as the fifteenth state in 1792, but it was just across the river from Indiana, a free state, so slavery developed differently in the Bluegrass State than it did in the Deep South. Kentucky's cash crops—tobacco and hemp—were less labor-intensive than the cotton or sugar grown in Louisiana or the Mississippi Delta. Kentucky farmers had no need for the large plantations that were the norm farther south. In fact, it became common practice to sell unwanted slaves. The term "sold down the river" is believed to have originated in the commonwealth because Kentucky farmers often sold unruly or unneeded slaves to be sent to harsher conditions on large plantations in the Deep South. Slave traders actually went from farm to farm looking to buy bondsmen to resell for a profit. By 1850, Louisville was shipping two to four thousand slaves to work in the harsh conditions of the Deep South.

Signature jugs from the National Jug Band Jubilee. The organization puts on a free, all-day festival celebrating jug band music. *Photo by Brian Bohannon, courtesy of the National Jug Band Jubilee.*

Rice Ballard, a Virginia slave trader, did business in Kentucky and retired to Louisville in the 1840s. According to Edward E. Baptist's article "Cuffy, Fancy Maids, and One-Eyed Men: Rape, Commodification, and the Domestic Slave Trade in the United States," Ballard and his partners were, at one point, shipping one thousand people a year to New Orleans. Ballard also illustrates the kind of wealth that was situated in Louisville. Again, according to Baptist, "with almost a thousand slaves to his name, Ballard had clambered to a pinnacle of wealth occupied by only a handful of others in the antebellum United States."

Illustrating the contradicting extremes that are the norm in Louisville, the city was also an important stop on the Underground Railroad. The Ohio River symbolized freedom in the eyes of the slaves because it was the dividing line between self-determination and bondage. Slaves referred to it as the "River Jordan" in spirituals because it was the finish line to independence.

Louisville has always had a small but consistent free black population. Prior to the Civil War, the number of free blacks and slaves accounted for 26 percent of the city's total population at its peak, and the percentage would never reach that high point after the war. Between 1830 and 1860, the number of free blacks grew from 232 to 1,917. The 1860 census also listed close to 5,000 slaves. These were the vessels of folk culture. Free and slave musicians often provided entertainment for the white population in Kentucky. The Kentucky Slave Narratives from the Federal Writers' Project of the Works Progress Administration include many examples of this. The story of Uncle Dick is typical of the patronizing but informative stories. It reported:

> *Uncle Dick, a negro servant of one of the Hendersons, was the fiddler of the neighborhood at weddings, husking parties and dances. Dick's presence was essential. Uncle Dick was fully aware of his own importance, and in consequence assumed a great deal of dignity in his bearing. Before setting out he always dressed himself with the greatest nicety. At the appointed time he was at the place with all the weight of his dignity upon him. Woe to the "darkies" who violated any of the laws of etiquette in his presence.*
>
> *On a certain evening there was to be a grand wedding festival among the colored gentry on a farm about six miles from Uncle Dick's residence. He was, of course called upon to officiate as master of ceremonies. He donned his long-tailed blue coat, having carefully polished the glittering gilt buttons; then raised his immense shirt collar, which he considered essential to his dignity, and, fiddle in hand, sallied forth alone. The younger folk had set out sometime before; but Uncle Dick was not to be hurried out of his dignity.*

The blues is usually associated with the cotton fields of Mississippi, but the black river roustabout working on the Ohio River also contributed to the genre. One popular song associated with the river is "Stagger Lee," a rock-and-roll hit for Lloyd Price in 1959. Price's recording was based on the blues standard "Stagolee," which deals with the killing of a gambler called Billy Lyons by the admitted bad man and pimp of the title. But the song probably evolved from a folk tune passed around by riverboat roustabouts. It is thought that the song's title, "Stagolee," refers to the *Stacker Lee*, a steamboat built by the Howard Shipyard in Jeffersonville, Indiana.

The *Stacker Lee* was owned by the Lee Line Steamers, and it ran between St. Louis and Memphis. The packet was rumored to offer on-board prostitution, and it was said that conditions onboard were so tough that one of the black laborers died every day. Mary Packet, author of *Steamboatin' Days: Folk Songs of the River Packet Era*, found three versions of "Stacker Lee" circulating among the riverboat workers. She believes the bad man in the blues song might have been a black roustabout who worked on the ship. Packet says, "Among Negro songs that are not associated with the Ohio River we find mention of another lawless character called 'Stagolee.' A comparison of many of these songs indicate that there is some connection [with the] *Stacker Lee*, either in truth or in legend."

Another chronicler of black music in early Louisville was Mildred J. Hill, one of the authors of "Happy Birthday to You." Hill was a musician, composer and pioneering ethnomusicologist who was born into a wealthy Louisville family on June 27, 1859. Her father was Reverend William Wallace Hill, a Presbyterian minister and director of the Bellewood Female Seminary during the Civil War. Mildred collaborated with her kindergarten teacher sister Patty on the book *Song Stories for the Kindergarten*, which was published in 1893. One of their songs, "Good Morning to All," provided the melody for "Happy Birthday."

Mildred is also responsible for one of the first musical histories of Louisville. Her "History of Music in Louisville" was part of the larger *Memorial History of Louisville*. In her article, Hill talks about the various music societies and dance halls that were created by the wealthy elite of the new city. But she also pays special attention to African American folk culture. Hill wrote:

> *Another branch of folk music which is already lost, is that of the roustabouts on the Mississippi and Ohio River steamboats. These negroes were with the whites constantly, but kept to themselves in a peculiar degree, and, therefore their music was untainted. It has all perished with the roustabouts themselves, and it is a great loss to the students of folklore.*

Hill was one of the first white Americans to realize the importance of African American music. "She went to black churches and sort of tried to write down all of these songs she was hearing sung," explains Robert Brauneis, author of *Copyright and the World's Most Popular Song*, which deals with "Happy Birthday." "If you can imagine what that was like in the 1880s and '90s, somebody doing that. It would be extremely unusual. I'm sure most white people would not find themselves in a black church on Sunday, let alone really paying attention to the music."

Mildred's transcriptions were published in a book called *Negro Hymns*. The original manuscript is at the University of Oregon. Most of the African American songs that were collected in the nineteenth century are of a religious nature because those are probably the things that blacks felt most comfortable sharing with white listeners. Hill also wrote an 1893 column for the *Louisville Courier-Journal* titled "Unconscious Composers," in which she discussed the musical cries of local street vendors. She wrote:

The street cries of our city are much more musical than those cities farther north and east; and will therefore be more valuable to musicians. It is the Negro who furnishes us with the most interesting street cries in this part of the country…He sings out his wares as though he enjoyed singing and didn't care whether business was brisk or not, and the characteristic plaintiveness is in them all.

There was a second school of black music in Louisville outside of the folk culture: the professional musician. With the increase in steamboats carrying passengers came a need for entertainment. This caused musicians to flock to Louisville. William H. Gibson Sr., a president of the Louisville Colored Musical Association, came to Louisville in 1847 from Baltimore. In the autobiographical sketch found in the *History of the United Brothers of Friendship and Sisters of the Mysterious Ten*, Gibson recorded:

During the forties and fifties was the golden age of steamboating on the Ohio and Mississippi rivers among the free colored men and women. Music was furnished on all the steamers for the passengers, and colored musicians were always in demand, as the foreigner had not monopolized everything in that line as now. The colored artist of those days made a respectable competency during the boating seasons. Musicians from the East would come West and South, as they were in demand.

A violinist named Henry Williams was the first black bandleader in Louisville. He came to the city around 1835. Williams ran a dancing school, and his band would provide the music for his students. In addition to dances at this school, Williams's band also performed at hotel balls, on steamboats and at other parties. Gibson remembered:

One among the colored artists in music was Henry Williams, the renowned violinist. But few distinguished white persons in the forties and fifties from whose parlors could not be heard the sonorous strains of Henry Williams' violin. He was employed to teach their sons and daughters quadrilles and mazourkas, and for years was the leading spirit of his profession.

Interesting enough, William's band was interracial. Gibson reports that the German immigrants had not learned the prejudice of other white Americans. This would change after the Civil War, when a large contingent of ex-Confederates moved to Louisville. After this, bands and most everything else would become segregated. A telling episode in Williams's life illustrates both the status and challenges of black musicians in nineteenth-century Louisville. It involves *Strader v. Graham*, a lawsuit filed in the Chancery Court of Louisville in 1844. Dr. Christopher Graham, who owned a popular resort in Harrodsburg, Kentucky, called Harrodsburg Springs, filed suit against the owners of the steamboat *Pike* for letting three of his slaves get away. The slaves were musicians named Henry, Reuben and George. The case is interesting to us because Henry and Rueben were supposed to be boarding with Williams when they ran away. Graham's deposition said:

> *This is to give liberty to my boys, Henry and Reuben, to go to Louisville, with Williams and to play with him till I may wish to call them home. Should Williams find it in his interest to take them to Cincinnati, New Albany, or any part of the South, even so far as New Orleans, he is at liberty to do so. I receive no compensation for their services except that he is to board and clothe them.*
>
> *My object is to have them well trained in music. They are young, one 17 and the other 19 years of age. They are both of good disposition and strictly honest, and such is my confidence in them that I have no fear that they will ever [act] knowingly wrong, or put me to trouble. They are slaves for life, and I paid for them an unusual sum; they have been faithful, hardworking servants, and I have no fear but that they will always be true to their duty, no matter in what situation they may be placed.*

Henry, Reuben and George got work in 1841 on the steamer the *Pike*, which operated on the 141 miles between Louisville and Cincinnati. Once in Ohio, the three slaves jumped ship and made their way to freedom in Canada. Graham held the ship's owners, Jacob Strader and James Gorman, responsible because they hired the musicians and took them aboard without his permission. He sought $1,500 for each slave. However, the court did not hold the steamboat liable because Graham had given the slaves permission to travel at their leisure. Williams was not implicated in the escape, although some people since then have felt he must have helped with the planning. Lucien Brown, a member of the Louisville Jug Band and blues singer Sara Martin's band, claimed Henry as a relative. Brown said the fiddler was his uncle. He related to jug band researcher John Randolph, "My grandmother told me the tale, and I read about it again, how the men ran off on the steamer *Pike* and were never seen again. But I had a cousin, a man lots older than I am, who used to get letters from him for a long time."

The largest white influence on Louisville music culture came from the Scots-Irish, who made up the largest portion of the city's population. In addition to their contribution of fiddle tunes and European dances, this group and the German immigrants were responsible for the city's brewing culture. Whiskey was being brewed in Louisville distilleries from the first decade, and to this day, Kentucky remains the top bourbon producer in the world. All of these distilleries provided work and made sure there were many empty whiskey jugs around for the early jug bands.

French immigrants were also an important component of the cultural atmosphere in Louisville. When the Virginia legislature incorporated the city in 1780, it was named for Louis XVI, the French monarch who was an ally in the American Revolution. Later, some of Louisville's most prominent families were descendants from French Huguenots or nobles who were fleeing the French Revolution that beheaded him. These French immigrants were deeply involved in the area's business community. A Frenchman named James Berthoud founded a small settlement called Shippingport on an Ohio River peninsula near the Falls of the Ohio. In 1820, Shippingport had a population of about five hundred people. Both Shippingport and Portland, another city on the other end of the Falls that was an early competitor to Louisville, had been absorbed into the River City by 1840. The French in the area were responsible for some of Louisville's first dance halls and classical ensembles.

The river traffic, especially contact with New Orleans, and the mix of cultures in Louisville were important factors in the formation of the early Louisville jug bands. Jug blowing first took hold among African American street bands, but it would slowly work its way to the city's white musicians. The Louisville sound reflected a cosmopolitan mix that combined the best of the South with influences from other cultures. But there is one other event in the development of jug music that was equally as important as the other factors. That was the invention of the minstrel show.

Chapter 3
Minstrel Shows and Ragtime

Although minstrels' strange and exaggerated gestures and makeup account for part of this appearance of distinctiveness, strong evidence exists that as part of their efforts to capture the native vitality of America and to establish themselves as authentic delineators of Negroes, white minstrels selectively adapted elements of black, as well as white, folk culture.
—*Robert Toll*, Blacking Up: The Minstrel Show in Nineteenth-Century America

One of the most influential figures in American history was born in Louisville, Kentucky, around 1830. Jim Crow would give his name to the restrictive segregation laws passed throughout the South after the Civil War, but he gained his initial fame on the stage. The character was the creation of a young actor named Thomas D. Rice. According to a 1932 *New York Times* retrospective on his career, "In 1828 he had the lead in 'The Mogul Tale' at the Lafayette Theatre and did so well that a portrait was made of him. For two years he played in stock companies in the South and the West. Then he discovered the Negro for the stage, and thereafter he was the most popular American actor of his time."

Rice, who was born in New York in 1808, is considered the father of the minstrel show. He specialized in slave roles. Dressed in blackface, he would entertain crowds by singing and dancing during a respite in the action. His characters rarely had anything to do with the actual plot of the production. Rice's breakthrough came in Louisville during the engagement

The Elmo Tucker Band performing at a Derby party at Hasenour's Restaurant. The jug player is Rudolph "Jazz Lips" Thompson, who also played in Whistler's Jug Band, the Henry Miles Jug Band and the Mutter Gutter Jug Band. *Courtesy of Gary Falk Audio.*

of *The Kentucky Rifle*, a melodrama that dealt with a young doctor wrongfully accused of murder. Behind the hotel where Rice's company was staying, there sat a livery stable owned by a man named Crow. It was there that Rice encountered a black man who would inspire his most popular character. In 1881, fellow actor Edmon S. Connor shared the story with the *New York Times*. Connor remembered:

> [Jim] *was very much deformed, the right shoulder being drawn high up, the left leg stiff and crooked at the knee, giving him a painful, but at the same time laughable limp. He used to croon a queer old tune with words of his own, and at the end of each verse would give a little jump, and when he came down he set his "heel a-rockin'." He called it "Jumping Jim Crow." The words of the refrain were,*

Wheel about, turn about
Do jis so
An ebery time I wheel about
Jump Jim Crow

Rice could have heard "Jumping Jim Crow" before encountering it in Louisville. The tune was derived from a well-known Irish ballad. The buzzard and crow imagery of the lyrics was also common in folktales. In the book *African Banjo Echoes in Appalachia*, Cecelia Conway even identified a Cajun version of the song that was sung in New Orleans. What was extraordinary about the performance Rice witnessed was the way the song was sung and the dance that went along with it. These were uniquely American and part of the black folk tradition. Conway found:

> *That the "Jim Crow" song text—and its refrain—was not simply an idiosyncratic performance by a slave from Louisville but had stanzas that remain part of a widespread oral tradition in the twentieth century further collaborates that the song had an African American folk source. Although the song no doubt passed from black folk to ministrels, and back to blacks in some cases, the material retained in the twentieth-century performances, hence presumably favored by these folks, gives some indication of what the song may have been like in the black folk tradition in the 1830s. Folk variations of "Jim Crow" showing only slight variations have been recorded in Texas, New Orleans, South Carolina, and three times in North Carolina.*

Rice was so taken with the slave's rendition of "Jumping Jim Crow" that he literally bought the clothes off his back. The actor then went to his hotel and wrote more verses for the song. Jim Crow, the character, debuted to an enthusiastic Louisville audience. Again, according to the *New York Times*, the spectators were so impressed that they called the actor back twenty times that night. The song "Jumping Jim Crow" became an international hit. Its success would make it possible for Rice to demand up to $100 a night performing the song and dance on the stages of Europe. Within the next decade after his character was born in Louisville, Jim Crow would inspire other minstrel icons like Sambo and Zip Coon. The popularity of the minstrel show led to the craze for coon songs like "All Coons Look Alike to Me" and "New Coon in Town" during the ragtime era and, later on, early vaudeville acts. Rice's creation of Jim Crow is important because it represents the first documented time that black song and dance caught the attention of mainstream America.

Percussion set for Y'uns Jug band. The group is a goodtime acoustic band blending jug band music with elements of folk, swing, country, blues and original material. *Photo by O'Neil Arnold, courtesy of the National Jug Band Jubilee.*

This pattern would repeat itself ad nauseam in American popular music from ragtime to hip-hop and in dances from the Charleston to twerking.

The minstrels traded in racial stereotypes and bigotry, but they were also unwitting vehicles of black culture. Minstrels like Dan Emmett were among the first whites to master the banjo, which had been brought with the slaves from Africa. Later minstrels followed Rice's pattern and based their performances on impersonating what they perceived as actual black folk culture. Yes, they exaggerated elements of it for comic relief, but many of them were faithful enough that even black audiences recognize the original source of some of the material.

Jug playing was one of those aspects of southern culture that was preserved by the minstrel tradition. It is not a surprise that the practice caught on in Louisville because the city was a major stop on the minstrel circuit. In his biography of Louisville-born composer and song collector John Jacob Niles, *I Wonder While I Wander*, author Ron Pen quotes from a diary entry where Niles describes a medicine show put on by one of his father's friends, Melrose D. Pankhurst. Niles recorded:

> *Pankhurst's show was actually a blackface minstrel show, except all the performers were truly negroes, all males and very talented. There were singers, pantomimes, a small group of actors who performed a hilarious after-piece called "A Wedding Breakfast in the Congo," and some expert soft-shoe dancers. And everyone, including the professor himself, could and did "double in brass" when the band played "Dixie."*

Niles, born in Louisville in 1892, was a major figure in the American folk revival. He understood the importance of the minstrel show to American culture. It is hard for modern people to fathom the popularity of minstrelsy, but it came along at a time when America was searching for a way to distance itself culturally from England after the War of 1812. Ironically, the minstrels also passed off some white southern and interracial entertainment as purely black culture. Many of the early minstrels were northern whites who were confused by the close relationship between blacks and whites in the South. This contributed to the further hybridization of American music as some southern practices were carried on by minstrel performers. In *Blacking Up: The Minstrel Show in 19ᵗʰ Century America*, Robert C. Toll stated:

> *Both South Carolina Negroes and white boatmen knew "Possum Up the Gum Tree"; Negro firemen on the Mississippi sang "Clare de Kitchen";*

and a Negro banjoist at a white frontier frolic in Tennessee in the early 1830s played "De Old Jaw Bone." Furthermore, black and white backwoodsmen both danced many of the same jigs and reels. The blend of Afro- and Euro-American musical and dance styles, which later became common in American popular culture, began on the frontier and was given wide exposure by the minstrels.

White actors dressing in blackface to play characters of African descent was not an American invention. English actors had been blacking up for years to play Othello and other black roles on the stage, but what was different in America was the unique cultural relationship between whites and blacks forged by the profound reality of slavery. Americans used blackface in a different way than Europeans. It justified slavery by depicting blacks as childlike and showing the comical situations that would arise if they were free. But the minstrel show also celebrated the distinctiveness of black song and dance. Europeans seemed to pick up immediately on the otherness of American culture. In 1822, an Englishman named Charles Matthews sang "Possum Up a Gum Tree" in black dialect in a show called *A Trip to America*, which documented his visit to the New World.

Minstrelsy became a way to spread new songs and clothing styles. There were actually white male actors who specialized in playing mulatto women who wore the latest fashions! The minstrel and medicine shows led to the creation of a repertoire of songs to which musicologist Tony Russell referred as the "common stock" because they influenced black and white songsters. These are old-time music standards like "Stagolee," "John Henry" and "In the Jailhouse." Today, most people know the latter song from the Coen brothers' movie *O' Brother Where Art Thou*.

"In the Jailhouse Now" was recorded by country legend Jimmie Rodgers and by Earl McDonald's Original Jug Band as "She's in the Graveyard Now." Rodgers was also a veteran of the medicine show. He wore blackface early in his career. His version of "In the Jailhouse" has some lyrical variations from McDonald's songs because they were passed down in different traditions— blues and country music. But it is obvious that the two tunes originated from the same source. Rodgers's version, which is aped by the Soggy Bottom Boys in the Coen brothers' movie, tells a comical tale about people thrown into jail because of their sins. Rodgers sang:

I had a friend named Ramblin' Bob
Who used to steal, gamble, and rob

He thought he was the smartest guy in town
But I found out last Monday
That Bob got locked up Sunday
They've got him in the jailhouse way down town.

Earl McDonald adds an element of satire. It is funny, but it also makes a sly political statement. It hails from a blues tradition pioneered by Blind Blake. McDonald starts out with imagery of a black man thrown in jail for voting too many times when black men could be killed for voting at all. Earl sang:

Now in the last election, when our folks weren't asked
They tried to get in a vote for President
I had a brother named Otis, a very swell promoter
He was always looking for swell advice
So, I told him to go right down to the polls and vote with his wholehearted soul
Instead of voting once, he voted twice
Now he's back in the jail, down in Louisville
The judge said he should have given him life.

He's in the jailhouse now, he's in the jailhouse now
We told that boy before he left home to leave those politics alone.

The message that voting could get blacks in trouble probably appealed to a white audience, but the black audience could also laugh at the overt political message at its center. Because it was often dangerous for African Americans to speak their minds, the culture is full of double meanings. Many scholars have written about the coded messages in the spirituals, where "Moses" could be Harriett Tubman or the "River Jordan" sometimes stood in for the Ohio River. But not as much attention has been paid to secular music, except maybe the double entendres found in blues lyrics. But even some children's songs hold elements of other messages. Most people are familiar with the chorus to the "Blue Tail Fly," even if they don't recognize the name of the song. It has been a popular children's chant on playgrounds and in classrooms for more than a century. The refrain went:

Jimmy crack corn, I don't care
Jimmy crack corn, I don't care
Jimmy crack corn, I don't care
Ole master has gone away.

Lawrence Levine pointed out that "Blue Tail Fly" represents the perspective of a slave taking "only slightly disguised pleasure in the death of a master." But to modern listeners, the lyrics may seem like nonsensical rhymes because they don't have a context for "cracking corn," which Levine says was a reference to making corn whiskey. Those slave songs that made fun of the masters particularly appealed to minstrels because Americans tend to enjoy making fun of their social elders. Levine wrote:

> *The themes common to so many of these antebellum songs make it clear that their continued popularity after slavery was only partly related to the strong ties of tradition. It is significant that a high proportion of the pre– and post–Civil War minstrel songs that lived on among black folks revolved around grievances against the master class.*

When African Americans joined the ranks of the minstrel show after 1840, they would have recognized in the music some elements of genuine black culture. They also accepted the mores established by earlier white minstrels. Gus Cannon, who played banjo with the Memphis Jug Band and Cannon's Jug Stompers, donned blackface to perform in traveling shows where he was billed as Banjo Joe. Cannon is best known for country blues tunes like "Poor Boy, Long Ways from Home" and "Walk Right In," which became a hit for the Rooftop Singers. He was born in 1883 in Red Banks, Mississippi, near Memphis, where he spent most of his career. In 1963, Cannon actually released a record on the city's Stax record label. In "Can You Blame Gus Cannon," a 2014 article for the *Oxford American* magazine, contemporary folk musician Don Flemons observed how black artists built on the minstrel tradition but used its tools to take their music in new directions. Flemons explained:

> *In his music I heard minstrelsy, but I could also hear a novel, legitimate black art form developed from minstrel roots. And not only that, Cannon's music was linked to both popular music and traditional blues and folk—he played country songs, he played popular songs, and he incorporated traditional music into his repertoire before there were any copyrights or industry standards for codifying song ownership. He played what he liked, it seems, though that's not to suggest that he wasn't influenced by a popular demand for minstrelsy entertainment. He was a professional musician, after all.*

The same can be said of many of the black songsters who appeared after the Civil War, including McDonald. Even when they followed white models, these artists brought a different perspective to the material. American scholars didn't pay much attention to black secular music until after the Civil War. When they did, they did not always appreciate its distinct features. Since some Negro spirituals and secular songs were based on European folk material, music writers assumed African American songs were just variations on these standards rather than original creations. But even the way the black artist performed the material set it apart. African American singing has direct links to vocal Africa. In fact, in *Myth of the Negro Past*, Melville Herskovitz identified it as African survival. Herskovitz concluded:

> *It is rare to find a Negro song, though quite European in melodic line, that is not tinged by some African-like modulation…In Guiana or Haiti or Brazil or the United States, other combinations are present; but it must be realized that they are combinations, all components of which must be weighted if we are to sense the developments that mark the syncretizing process…no matter how intense or how long was its contact with European melodies, it has in some measure persisted.*

The coon song came into vogue after the 1880s. Like the minstrel show before it, the coon song reinforced the idea of African Americans as inferior and buffoonish. The popularity of the genre coincided with the Reconstruction era, when some southern whites were worried about the social gains made by black Americans post–Civil War. But some of these coon songs were also popular among black audiences. In fact, coon songs gave us some of the most popular American composers, men like Stephen Foster, Irving Berlin and Louisville native William S. Hays, who claimed to have written the lyrics to "Dixie." The coon song era also boasted some of the earliest African American show business successes.

The 1896 hit "All Coons Look Alike to Me" was composed by a black man named Ernest Hogan. Born in Bowling Green, Kentucky, in 1865, Hogan started out in minstrel shows, but he would end up being the first black performer in a Broadway show. Hogan's "All Coons" was an adaptation of another song called "All Pimps Look Alike to Me." Another popular black composer was Irving Jones, who wrote "Under the Chicken Tree," which would be recorded by the Louisville Jug Band. It may seem strange that African Americans would be involved in something that demeaned their own people, but many of the black composers of coon songs did not see them as a true reflection of black people.

When the black songsters and jug bands started recording, coon songs would be part of their repertoire. But this genre is also important because it represented a new kind of sound. The coon song was a subgenre of the syncopated music known as ragtime, a form of proto-jazz that was pioneered in the African American dance halls of New Orleans and St. Louis. Today, most people associate it with the piano music of Scott Joplin, but that was a mature form of the music.

Ragtime lacked the improvisational elements of jazz. The music was usually based on sheet music. Ragtime would be a huge influence on Earl McDonald and other Louisville Jug Band musicians, who would often refer to their songs as "rags." One of the earliest popular ragtime composers was a man named Ben Harney, who had an 1895 hit with "You've Been a Good Old Wagon but You Done Broke Down." Harney was born in Louisville in 1872, and he is often referred to as the "Father of Ragtime" because he was the first to introduce the music to the New York stage. Harney claimed to have created the genre after seeing two African Americans playing banjos at a party in Louisville. In his article about the origins of the genre, "Louisville: Birthplace of Ragtime," N. David Williams points out that Harney grew up on the edge of the city's black community, and he undoubtedly listened to black musicians when he was growing up. Williams conjectured:

> *The word "rag" or ragtime probably derives from the early rag dances performed by black deck-hands while working up and down the Mississippi. But the one popular legend has it that the word actually comes from the saloons of Louisville.*

According to Williams, when Harney walked into Tom Johnson's dance hall at Tenth and Green Streets, the men would say, "Take off your rag, Ben, and play us those new songs." Eventually, whenever they saw him, they would simply say, "It's ragtime."

Harney, who died in 1928, is the subject of many rumors in Louisville. He played with interracial bands, and some black musicians were convinced that he was a black man passing as white. Earl Hines, the great New Orleans pianist who would also record with Clifford Hayes, said as much in his autobiography. There has been no conclusive proof that Harney had a black ancestor, but blues historian Paul Oliver took it as fact. In the book *Songster & Saints*, Oliver contends:

Another black composer who was "passing for white" was Ben Harney, whose "You've Been a Good Old Wagon but You Done Broke Down" and "Mister Johnson, Turn Me Loose" were widely acclaimed for their authenticity of idiom. But though the Harney title was recorded by Bessie Smith, neither Harney nor [Ernest] Hogan left any impact on black song such that their compositions appeared much on race records, and neither seems to have influenced black folk vocal traditions.

Again, there was no proof that Harney was anything other than what he presented to the world. But he was obviously influenced by black music in Louisville, which continued to develop along two streams until after the Civil War, when segregation forced the two schools together in the same bands. The folk culture was practiced by the common laborer, while professional musicians served the white and black masses on boats, at dances and at other social events.

After Henry Williams died, on Valentine's Day 1850, one of his former band members became the most popular bandleader in the city. Violinist James C. Cunningham was born in the West Indies. He served in the British navy before coming to Kentucky. Like Williams, he ran a dancing school that taught the children of Louisville's elite. Also like Williams, Cunningham had an interracial band that employed German immigrants. He was also reportedly a member of the Underground Railroad, which did not seem to impact his popularity with white audiences. His band performed for President-elect Zachary Taylor, who had a home in Louisville, and Sallie Ward, the queen of the Kentucky social scene. Cunningham also became one of the wealthiest African Americans in Louisville by the time he died in 1877.

Cunningham's son, cornet player James R. Cunningham, started Louisville's first brass band, the Falls City Brass Band. The younger Cunningham's band toured Europe and Japan and performed for Presidents U.S. Grant and Grover Cleveland and even Queen Victoria. By this time, the eve of the twentieth century, Louisville musicians were playing Dixieland jazz, the syncopated dance music from New Orleans to which Jelly Roll Morton referred as "hot music." The stage was set for the early jug bands.

Chapter 4
The Early Jug Bands

Most of the younger guys in the brass bands wanted to get out and swing, but the older guys used to prefer to stay with the marches.
—Dicky Wells, trombonist for Count Basie, who got his start at the Booker T. Washington Community Center in Louisville

The story of Louisville jug music actually begins in New Orleans, where spasm bands first appeared at the end of the nineteenth century. These amateur groups consisted mostly of children playing homemade instruments. Although spasm bands started among African American musicians, the most famous of them was a white group called the Razzy Dazzy Spasm Band. It was founded around 1895 by an enterprising newsboy named Emile "Stalebread Charlie" Lacoume, who recruited other newsboys between the ages of twelve and fifteen for the group. They worked the streets of Storyville, New Orleans's famous red-light district, playing a potent mixture of folk songs, ragtime and blues on instruments like a bass crafted from a half-barrel strung with clothesline and played with a bow made out of cypress stick, a banjo made from a cheese box and a guitar from a soap box. The musicians also sported memorable nicknames; in addition to Stale Bread, there was Warm Gravy, Pork Chop and Chinee, to name just a few.

In his famous Library of Congress interview with Alan Lomax, published as *Mr. Jelly Roll*, the New Orleans pianist Jelly Roll Morton remembered, "A lot of bad bands that we used to call spasm bands played any jobs they could get in the streets. They did a lot of ad-libbing in ragtime style with different

A jug band outside Hanson Motors in Louisville. Businesses would use jug bands to attract customers. *Courtesy of the University of Louisville Photographic Archives & Special Collections.*

solos in succession, one guy would get tired and let another musician have the lead."

Not all spasm bands were "bad bands." In fact, the best of them were pretty good. Some people, including Lacoume himself, considered the Razzy Dazzy Spasm Band to be the first real jazz group. At the very least, the spasm groups influenced cornetist Buddy Bolden, the forefather of the sound that would be perpetuated by King Oliver, Louis Armstrong and generations of other New Orleans musicians.

The cultural influence of New Orleans led to the appearance of local spasm bands in towns along the Mississippi and Ohio Rivers. In *The Creation of Jazz*, Burton W. Peretti observed, "New Orleans was at the base of a lattice of port cities along the Mississippi and Ohio River valleys, including Baton Rouge, Memphis, St. Louis, Minneapolis, Louisville and Cincinnati. The similarities in the black music of these cities often outweighed their differences."

Because of riverboat traffic and travel on the Louisville & Nashville Railroad, people were moving back and forth between the cities. This led to string and brass bands developing in places like Louisville and Cincinnati at the same time they did in New Orleans. Louisville, St. Louis, Cincinnati and New Orleans would all be home to jug bands, which were essentially just spasm bands with a jug player handling the bass parts.

Part of the reason that the spasm band became so popular in Louisville is because there were so many more opportunities for musicians in the city after the Civil War. Louisville experienced economic and population booms in the fifty years following the war. The city's population went from 68,033 in 1860 to more than 200,000 people by 1910. Many of these new arrivals were ex-Confederates in search of jobs and business opportunities that came from trade. They had a great impact on the city's culture and political life, as Louisville, which had been a Union stronghold during the war, became home to chapters of the United Confederate Veterans and the United Daughters of the Confederacy, which erected a Confederate Civil War monument at Second Street in 1895.

Kentucky was a neutral state in the Civil War, but it raced to join the Lost Cause after it was over. In *Life Behind a Veil: Blacks in Louisville, Kentucky, 1865–1930*, George Wright documents some of the changes this wrought in the city's culture. Wright wrote:

> *Historians have accurately labeled Reconstruction in Kentucky "Confederacy Supremacy." A recent scholar of Louisville called the influx of ex-Confederates into the city "remarkable." It seems that a part of the*

"rite of passage" into the business world of the city was to have been an officer in the Confederacy. Nearly all Louisville's journalists, lawyers, realtors, and merchants were former rebels.

The influx of ex-Confederates also had an impact on the other major group of new Louisville residents: African Americans. During the Civil War, many slaves traveled to Louisville in search of freedom since it was a Union garrison. After the war, the freedmen continued to gravitate to the city looking to reconnect with family or to find work on the river or the railroad during the first wave of black migration from rural areas to urban centers. Louisville's black population was 14,956 in 1870, but it had grown to 40,087 by 1910.

Before the Civil War there were pockets of African Americans all over the city. Due to the rising pro-Confederacy sentiment that dominated the city at the end of the nineteenth century, African Americans increasingly found themselves limited to segregated communities. The oldest black settlement was west of downtown in the Parkland neighborhood, which was known locally as "Little Africa" after 1894. Smoketown was located southeast of downtown. In the east, along English Station Road, there was an African American community called Berrytown. There was also a black cultural hub similar to Beale Street in Memphis along Louisville's Walnut Street, which is now Muhammad Ali Boulevard. This is where people would find clubs and other black-run businesses.

By 1900, Louisville had a large pool of folk and professional musicians who performed on the riverboats and at various events for black and white audiences. At the time, Louisville was one of the twenty top cities in America, and the city's wealth opened up new opportunities for musicians. The week of the Kentucky Derby, which was run for the first time in 1875, was always a chance for anyone with talent to make a few extra bucks.

There is a rather famous photo of a Louisville spasm band in the University of Louisville Photo Archives. The picture captures four African American teens in a dirt yard. The tallest boy is to the right holding a jug. Next to him is a smaller boy with a piece of pipe that has been twisted to resemble a saxophone. Another boy is sitting at a makeshift drum set, next to someone holding a ukulele. This photograph is from the 1920s, but groups like this would have been a common sight in 1890s Louisville. Ralph Helm, aka Roscoe Goose of the Juggernaut Jug Band, has suggested that the jug player in the picture is Rudolph Thompson, who played with Whistler's Jug Band and the Henry Miles Jug Band. When he was a boy, Thompson

A jug band class.
*Courtesy of the
University of Louisville
Photographic Archives &
Special Collections.*

played in the street with the Mud Gutter Jug Band, a spasm group made up of boys under twelve years old. Thompson blew a glass jug, and the group also included William Bean on spoons; Curtis Williams on stone jug; and Ambrose Williams playing a mud gutter, which was a drainpipe with a kazoo inside. After 1926, the group added James Olden on washboard and singer Leon Burks.

Drummer John Harris, who played with Earl McDonald's Ballad Chefs, also played in a similar spasm group that worked the streets for money. Harris was born in 1907 near Louisville in LaGrange, Kentucky. Harris remembers:

> *Now the kids' bands, the streets was the only place they played, just on the streets, play for nickels and dimes. They wouldn't allow them to go into the saloons. The only thing a kid could do, he could play on the streets like that and like some guys had money and was in a hotel, they would take them up to those hotel rooms and have them playing and dancing and singing all night and they'd make plenty of money; they really make money. Yeah, they take them up there. The hotel manager never would bother, 'cause the big shot had money; they could do what they wanted.*
>
> *The Frank Fehr Brewery would hire kids' bands to play on the streets. They would outfit 'em in fancy, bright red uniforms that had "Fehr's Beer" in big letters on the front and the back and even on the caps. One year I couldn't get a job playing drums on the streets so I lined up four boys: there was two guitars, a washboard and spoons, and I played comb. They hired us and we played on the streets for a few days when the man that hired us heard us play—we were really terrible—and fired us on the spot. We got three dollars a day each, and that was good money. Old Man Fehr wouldn't use older musicians because they'd go into the saloons and get drunk, and everybody in the place would be hollering for a free round of drinks.*

Most of what is known about the early Louisville jug bands is due to Harris and two other men, Fred Cox and John Randolph. Harris and Randolph helped Cox gather material for his unpublished manuscript for a book called *The Jug Bands of Louisville*. Cox was an Indianapolis attorney and a collector of early jazz records. In 1950, he was working for the Indiana State Employment Office, where he got into a conversation with an elderly African American man who had moved to Indianapolis from Dallas, Texas. Cox asked the man if there were many jazz bands around Texas when he was younger. The man answered, "Yes, there was jazz bands around all right, but I never heard any of them because they played only at white functions, but I'll tell you one thing that I did hear there—that was a jug band. Man, that was something."

The conversation piqued Cox's interest. He went to a friend, who collected old 78s, and asked him about jug bands. After hearing the Dixieland Jug Blowers for the first time, the attorney became an apostle for jug music. With the help of Harris and Randolph, another musician, he began interviewing jug band players and amassing an exceptional repository of photographs, oral histories, newspaper clippings and posters. Cox died before he could finish writing his manuscript, but his work was serialized in a British blues magazine called *Storyville*. The information was also compiled into a pamphlet, called *The Jug Bands of Louisville*, by the magazine's publisher.

The earliest jug band that Cox could find was the Cy Anderson Jug Band, which featured B.D. Tite on jug. Tite came from a family of Louisville musicians; his father, James Tite, was a renowned fiddler, and his brother, William Tite, was a banjo player who led a popular string band. The information gathered by Cox, Harris and Randolph was mostly anecdotal because it came from later jug band musicians.

According to Cox, B.D. Tite and a man named Dan Smith, who was called Black Daddy, found themselves in the Appalachian Mountains of southwestern Virginia looking for work in the late 1890s. Someone told them that Cy Anderson, a fiddler whose family had a string band, might be looking for a banjo player, and they headed up to his home. The two musicians hit it off with Anderson and decided to stay with him for a few weeks. According to Cox, this was the first time Tite saw someone playing the jug:

> *One summer evening the band was warming up on the front porch. A few neighbors had wandered over, listening quietly; down the lane came an elderly colored man carrying a jug. The Andersons nodded to him as he sat on the edge of the porch and began to lay down a simple bass line behind the music blowing on the jug. B.D. stopped playing, sat near the jug blower, watching and listening, fascinated by the sounds he was hearing for the first time. When the band finished the tune, B.D. was all questions, but the old man could only say, "I just picked it up and started blowing." The only advice he would offer was simple enough: "Look around for the right jug; a jug is a jug if you want whiskey, but if you want to blow on it find one that's got music in it."*

It is hard to say how much of the Tite story is true and how much is romantic imagination. No one is around to deny or confirm the details. It is likely that Tite came across jug playing earlier than Cox says he did, considering how widespread the practice was in the South. What we do know is that Tite convinced the Cy Anderson group to go to Louisville, where it spent years working in the city and on riverboats spreading the gospel of jug music. Cox wrote:

> At the turn of the century, Louisville was the southern terminus of a ragtime circuit that included Indianapolis and Chicago. Ragtime pianists were constantly coming and going up or down the line. In order to get in on some of the action, [the jug band] used the first trick of the street bands: stop in front of a busy white saloon from which sounds could be heard, and begin playing their jug band music. After a while the saloon patrons would be attracted by their music and would drift outside for a better hearing. When a goodly number of his drinking customers had come out, the shopkeeper would be incensed enough to come out himself and invite the band to play inside in order to get his paying customers back inside buying drinks…At the black saloons they would simply walk in with their instruments, sit at a table sipping beer while listening to the music. Sooner or later they would be asked to play and the owner would provide free drinks for the band if the crowd liked them.

The Cy Anderson Jug Band spent seven years, from 1902 to 1909, working as entertainment on riverboats. Cox describes it as the Johnny Appleseed of jug music. The music the group played was probably just a traditional variation of string band material, popular tunes and blues. The next generation of Louisville jug musicians would build on this foundation, adding jazz instrumentation to the jug band toolkit.

Opposite, top: A jug band performing at Meades Landing Farm in 1955 at a party for a ballet group. *Courtesy of the family.*

Opposite, bottom: A jug band performing at a Wood-Mosaic Derby Party in 1967 at a farm owned by Paul MacLean. *Courtesy of the family.*

Terri Brown, granddaughter of Earl McDonald, on stage for the induction of the Dixieland Jug Blowers into the Jug Band Hall of Fame, September 2011. *Photo by Brian Bohannon, courtesy of the National Jug Band Jubilee.*

Above and opposite, bottom: Members of the Old Southern Jug Blowers from Kansai, Japan, at the 2009 Jubilee. The group has recorded two CDs of Earl McDonald songs. *Photo by O'Neil Arnold, courtesy of the National Jug Band Jubilee.*

Daniel Pickle of the Deep Fried Pickle Project, 2009 Jubilee. The band performs at family-friendly concerts on homemade instruments made out of recycled materials. *Photo by O'Neil Arnold, courtesy of the National Jug Band Jubilee.*

A participant in a jug-blowing seminar at the National Jug Band Jubilee. The festival offers lessons on jug blowing and playing the saw. *Photo by Brian Bohannon, courtesy of the National Jug Band Jubilee.*

A poster promoting the National Jug Band Jubilee. The festival has celebrated jug band music since 2005. *Photo by Brian Bohannon, courtesy of the National Jug Band Jubilee.*

The Ballard Chefs at a public performance. The group toured the Southwest promoting Ballard & Ballard Flour Company. *Courtesy of the University of Louisville Photographic Archives & Special Collections.*

Left: Jim Kweskin, former leader of Kweskin's Jug Band, at the 2010 National Jug Band Jubilee. Kweskin was one of the leaders of the American folk revival. *Photo by Brian Bohannon, courtesy of the National Jug Band Jubilee.*

Below: Part of the J.C. Barnett Collection at the Oldham County Historical Society. Barnett collected hundreds of antique bourbon jugs. *Photo by Brian Bohannon.*

Right: Eric "Hambone" Buhrer of the Cincinnati Dancing Pigs. This group performed at the first National Jug Band Jubilee. *Photo by Brian Bohannon, courtesy of the National Jug Band Jubilee.*

Below: Jubilee friend Fred Glock blowing some jug. The retired chemist was an original member of the Juggernaut Jug Band. *Photo by O'Neil Arnold, courtesy of the National Jug Band Jubilee.*

Y'uns Jug Band percussionist J. Miller. *Photo by O'Neil Arnold, courtesy of the National Jug Band Jubilee.*

Right: Geoff Muldaur at the 2010 National Jug Band Jubilee. Muldaur was a founding member of Jim Kweskin's Jug Band. He was inducted into the Jug Band Hall of Fame. *Photo by Brian Bohannon, courtesy of the National Jug Band Jubilee.*

Below: Bradley Selz of Boo Bradley on stage with workshop participants at the 2011 National Jug Band Jubilee. The group is a hot blues stompin', jelly roll jumpin', rag jazz infusin' and acoustic jug attack from Madtown, Wisconsin. *Photo by Brian Bohannon, courtesy of the National Jug Band Jubilee.*

Chapter 5

Earl McDonald and the Golden Age of Jug Bands

A good jug player has to learn to play by ear and keep time. If he gets off the time, he throws the whole band off.
—Rudolph Thompson, jug player for the Mud Gutter Jug Band and the Henry Miles Jug Band

What is probably the earliest published account of the Louisville Jug Band doesn't actually mention the group by name. On October 20, 1914, the *Louisville Courier-Journal* reported, "Jug Band Arrested on Complaints Against Noise." The accompanying article explained that Ben Calvin, John Smith and Earl McDonald were charged with disorderly conduct after residents on Market Street, between First and Second, complained that the three musicians were making noise after midnight. It is doubtful that the newspaper reporter—or the arresting officer, for that matter—even knew or cared that the men were members of the Louisville Jug Band. The group was still ten years away from the seminal recordings that would make its name nationally known and spawn a jug band recording craze.

In 1914, the Louisville Jug Band was just one of many black string bands dotting the South, although it was one that usually played at high-society functions and not street venues. The group was among the earliest and the most successful of the second generation of jug bands that followed the Cy Anderson Jug Band.

Between 1900 and 1930, there were a great number of active jug bands working the streets of Louisville. Researchers Fred Cox, John Randolph

The Ballard Chefs in front of a WHAS Radio microphone. Earl McDonald is holding the jug. The group's show lasted from 1929 to 1932. *Courtesy of the University of Louisville Photographic Archives & Special Collections.*

and John Harris documented more than thirty of them featuring Louisville musicians. In addition to McDonald's various outfits, there were Whistler's Jug Band, Phillip's Louisville Jug Band, the Henry Smith Jug Band, the Hooks Tilford Jug Band and Charlie Anderson's Jug Band. Even more bands came from out of town on a regular basis to make some quick money on the streets of Louisville.

"They had a lot of clubs, all the way from Sixth on down to Twenty-fifth, before they tore down Walnut Street," fiddler Henry Miles told *Living Blues* in 1982.

> *Some guys come in here from different places that played harps and like that. Hang out, hit right here, to Sixth & Walnut. That was the headquarters. Poolrooms and them things, and they'd hit right through here, some would get jobs. They'd stay here maybe one or two days and then jump up and go somewhere else. Like the Derby was one reason they come. See, they made good money. They'd make good tips. The*

Derby, that's where people from everywhere come to Louisville. White and colored. It's a money town.

The musicians who made up the nucleus of the Louisville jug band scene recorded together in various combinations under several monikers: Sara Martin's Jug Band, Old Southern Jug Band, Clifford's Louisville Jug Band, the Dixieland Jug Blowers and Earl McDonald's Original Louisville Jug Band. Jug player Earl McDonald was one of the constants in all these groups. Because of his versatility, McDonald was without a doubt the greatest jug blower of his generation. He was proficient enough in old-time music and blues music to play with country legend Jimmie Rodgers ("My Good Gal's Gone Blues"), but he could also swing in a jazz setting with the likes of clarinetist Johnny Dodds ("House Rent Rag," among others), a renowned Louis Armstrong sideman. McDonald was also a charming vocalist, comedian and bandleader. The music he made was full of vaudeville humor and top-rate musicianship. Jug music is sometimes called "good-time" music because it is celebratory. It is, after all, dance music, and the musicians knew how to move a crowd.

Miles played fiddle for McDonald in one of his later groups, the Ballard Chefs. He credited McDonald's skill on the jug with innate musicianship and knowledge of different genres. "We played blues, swing tunes, marches," he told the *Living Blues*. "All kinds of songs. 'My Old Kentucky Home,' that was their [the Ballard Chef's] theme song. The whole band sung. Earl could sing this blues—jug players, they kept up with the blues stuff. Earl played piano, played drums, played bass, too."

McDonald's music was steeped in the minstrel show tradition; he was born just one generation away from slavery. He came into the world on October 2, 1885, in South Carolina, although he moved to Louisville with his mother, Mattie, and grandmother when he was still a toddler. The family accompanied a man named McDonald, who was their employer. It was not unusual for former slaves to continue working for the families who once held them in bondage. This seems to have been the relationship between Earl's family and their employer, a former plantation owner, since they shared a name and seemed to have a close relationship. In *The Jug Bands of Louisville*, Fred Cox wrote:

One afternoon in October, Mr. McDonald came home early. Hearing music coming from the parlour, he asked his housekeeper, Mattie, what was going on. Apologetically, she replied that it was her fault; Earl had organized a little band that was playing on the streets and she had forbidden him to do anymore street playing. She explained that she had given the boys permission to use the parlour after school. Mr. McDonald quietly walked over to the closed doors and quietly walked in. The boys were aghast at this unexpected intrusion. Mr. McDonald smiled and assured them he had no objection to their using the parlour for rehearsals.

Earl discovered the jug as an instrument after hearing the Cy Anderson Jug Band playing on the street in 1900. He was already learning to play the bass horn and the string bass, but he became a quick disciple of B.D. Tite, who probably gave him some pointers on handling the jug. He founded the first Louisville Jug Band in 1902 as a street band. With the assistance of his mother's employer, the group began playing at house parties given by the city's white elite, who would become a regular source of employment for his group. Cox suggests that Judge Robert Worth Bingham, publisher of the *Louisville Courier-Journal*, was an early patron, and another longtime fan was Sally Brown, wife of Brown-Forman liquor heir W.L. Lyons Brown. These connections help explain why, in 1903, the Louisville Jug Band became the first jug band to perform at the Kentucky Derby. Having a jug band at the Derby would remain a Churchill Downs tradition well into the 1930s.

McDonald was among the most stable of the jug band musicians. He appears in most of the Louisville city directories published in his lifetime. When he wasn't playing jug music, he worked as a waiter or a common laborer. Interestingly enough, it's on McDonald's 1917 draft registration card where he first describes himself as a musician. At the time, he was living at 1224 Carpet Alley, which would remain his address until 1931. The home was a regular stomping ground for other jug band musicians, and it inspired the Dixieland Jug Blowers' song "Carpet-Alley Breakdown," which was also among the tracks that featured Dodds.

Not much is known about McDonald's first wife, Mary, but she seems to have also been a musician. The couple had a daughter, noted civil rights activist Mattie Mathis. She remembered her mother in an interview with David Cline for the Southern Oral History Program:

She was originally from Georgia, and she never wanted to go back to Georgia. I don't know what experience she had. She was born like in 1899, and I don't know what happened. But she was a singer…She sang with Mahalia Jackson. Yeah, in '52, Mother's Day. I'll never forget that. Of course, that's the year she died, in August. But on Mother's Day at

Memorial Auditorium, she sang with Mahalia Jackson. I got to get onstage and meet Miss Jackson. That was the biggest thrill.

Mattie did not have as much to say about her father, who did not seem to play a large role in her life. Mattie's children say she never talked about her father's connection to jug music, and she was amused when people came around asking about it. Mattie was still a teenager when Earl died, and he had separated from her mother. However, according to her children, Mattie had a good relationship with his second wife, Laura.

In addition to his talent on the jug, McDonald was an excellent organizer and support system for other musicians. This is illustrated by the fact that he tended to have long-term relationships with the people who worked with him. Ben Calvin, the mandolin player arrested with McDonald in 1914, was a longtime collaborator. He joined the Louisville Jug Band in 1907 and played with it until he left town in 1916. Calvin was also a member of McDonald's Ballard Chefs.

Guitarist John Smith, the other person arrested that night in 1914, was probably a member of the musically inclined Smith family of southern Indiana. There were six brothers who played music, including noted guitarist/banjo player Cal Smith. By all accounts, Cal could have had a great career if not for heavy drinking. He played with most of McDonald's outfits and with the W.C. Handy Orchestra. He was only thirty-four when he died in 1937. Ralph S. Helm, jug player for the Juggernaut Jug Band, says guitarist Ed Chestnut, who also played with McDonald, had fond memories of Cal Smith.

"I sat with Ed Chestnut over in his basement in New Albany, and we talked about the old jug band guys," Helm told me in an interview.

He said Cal Smith may have been a little afraid to go out and travel. Cal seriously could have been another Lonnie Johnson, but bigger because he was in that jazzy era. He could have gone to New York and been the forerunner of someone like Charlie Christian, maybe. Ed told me that every black band—Count Basie, Duke Ellington, Jimmy Lunceford, even Benny Goodman's people—whenever they were in Louisville they were all looking for Cal. They all wanted to go hear him play. I believe him. When you listen to those old recordings with him on banjo or guitar, he was that good.

The Smiths were related to another family of musicians, the Hayes brothers. The clan included Curtis, a guitar and banjo player, and Clifford,

a fiddler who was McDonald's main collaborator. The family originated from Glasgow, Kentucky, which they left for Jeffersonville, Indiana, in 1912. Curtis and Clifford had a string band with their brothers, Otis and Sydney.

Clifford Hayes is a tragic figure in jug music because he felt pigeonholed by the genre. Throughout his career, he attempted to break out of the jug band ghetto by playing straight-ahead jazz or combining jazz and country music without the jug in groups like Clifford Hayes's Orchestra and the Louisville Stompers. But jug music was what people wanted from him. During the Depression, Clifford had to go back to featuring a jug player in his group, in part because of the popularity of McDonald's Ballard Chefs, which had a popular radio show on WHAS Radio and traveled the country promoting Ballard & Ballard Flour Company.

The Ballard Chefs. The group included many former members of Earl McDonald's Original Louisville Jug Band. *Courtesy of the University of Louisville Photographic Archives & Special Collections.*

Born in 1893, Clifford was the second oldest of the Hayes boys. He joined McDonald in the Louisville Jug Band in 1914 and collaborated with him off and on until the early 1930s. By the time Hayes joined, the group had already started making excursions to bigger cities. A Broadway producer who had seen the jug band at a Derby party arranged for a stint at Hippodrome Theater in New York. The group also played the Lamb's Café in Chicago. These would be the first of many trips to the Big Apple and the Windy City.

Clifford was one of the few jug band musicians who made a living solely through music. The 1930 census shows him living in Jeffersonville with his wife, Sareida, and his mother, Susie. He lists his occupation as a musician at a theater. Clifford is not remembered as a great innovator of his instrument like Cal Smith, but he was a prolific songwriter and bandleader. He collaborated with a number of other performers outside of Louisville, including a Cincinnati blues musician named Kid Coley ("Tricks Ain't Walkin' No More") and several New Orleans players.

Clifford was also known for shady dealings. One of the reasons the Louisville jug musicians recorded under so many different names was because they would sign contracts with multiple record companies at the same time. Clifford was known to try to cheat other musicians out of their equal share of a night's pay. He would tell his band mates that they were being paid less than they were and then pocket the difference. This untrustworthiness with money and battles over who should get credit for the success of their various projects would lead to a falling out between Clifford and Earl McDonald around 1920. After this, the two continued to hire each other as sidemen for particular recording dates or club shows but worked together only with strict agreements. This was probably the case in 1924, when the Louisville Jug Band headed to New York for a club stint and ended up going into the studio with Louisville-born blues singer Sara Martin.

After the success of "Crazy Blues" for Okeh Records prompted the creation of "race" record category in 1920, record companies scrambled to sign a roster of black, vaudeville-trained singers. Two of the earliest were from Louisville: Martin and Edith Goodall Wilson, the latter of whom is remembered mostly as an actress. Born in 1896, Edith was Kingfish's mother-in-law on the *Amos 'n' Andy* radio show and portrayed Aunt Jemima for many years. In fact, the iconic image on the pancake mix is supposed to have been modeled after Wilson. Her singing career began in Louisville in 1919 at a local theater. She was soon part of a trio with her husband, pianist Danny Wilson, and his sister, Lena. In 1921, she signed to Columbia Records and recorded a few Perry Bradford songs with Johnny Dunn's Jazz

Hounds. Bradford always felt that he didn't get enough credit for writing "Crazy Blues," so he was more involved with Wilson's initial recordings.

The number of future jazz and blues performers who hailed from Louisville in the early part of the twentieth century is proof of the city's rich music culture. In addition to Wilson and Martin, the city produced Ford L. Washington and John W. Sublett, who formed the seminal vaudeville tap dancing duo Buck and Bubbles; trombonist Dickie Wells; bebop trumpeter Jonah Jones; bluesmen John "Preacher" Stephens and Sylvester Weaver; drummer Elmo Dunn, Martin's younger brother; and jazz singer Helen Humes. Many of these performers got their starts playing at the Booker T. Washington Community Center, which had a marching band for African American children led by Bessie Miller Allen.

"I can't remember anybody much that was in show business that went to school with me, although Jonah [Jones] I knew because he lived around the corner from me," Wilson told Daphne Duval Harrison, author of *Black Pearls: Blues Queens of the 1920s*. "There were programs and recitals in churches and clubs. All of those kinds of things are still going on there…They used to have little kids give shows and have all of them do different things, and all like that. Because I've been singing since I was two years old."

This was the culture that produced Martin, who was older and a more successful singer than Wilson. Martin was born in 1884 to William and Katie Dunn. She was already an accomplished singer when Wilson was still a child. Wilson told Harrison:

> *I didn't know* [Sara Martin] *very good, but I knew about her because she was singing back in Louisville, you know, about then, and the reason I knew about her at all is when I started to learn songs, this boy, Jimmy Clark, and his brother, Joe Clark, put on shows and Jimmy played piano. Well, they had people come over to their house and rehearse, and I used to go play with his sister, and I'd hear these people rehearsing, and that's how I heard Sara. And I used to go in after they left and imitate them, you know, singing songs and stuff.*

Martin started out working the black vaudeville circuit. At one time, she was the highest-paid black performer in America. She was already a big name on stage when she signed to Okeh Records, which billed her as the "Black Sophie Tucker" and the "Famous Moanin' Mama," a reference to Columbia Records' Clara Smith, "Queen of the Moaners." Martin had a string of hits with New Orleans composer Clarence Williams, including "Sugar Blues" and "Uncle Sam Blues." She also happened to be the first person to record the jazz standard "Ain't Nobody's Business If I Do." In addition to her work with Okeh, she recorded for other companies under the names Margaret Johnson and Sally Robinson. She appeared in the 1923 film *Hello Bill* with dancer Bill "Bojangles" Robinson and the following year was in the first talking picture with an all-black cast. At the end of her career, Martin would try to transition to gospel music. She even recorded with Thomas A. Dorsey, godfather of the genre. Dorsey had made a similar transition from a blues musician named Georgia Tom to being a sanctified artist, but the gospel audience would not accept Martin. She retired to Louisville, where she ran a nursing home until her death in 1955.

As a singer, Martin was a moaner in the Bessie Smith tradition. She was at the height of her popularity in September 1924, when she made the recordings that introduced the world to jug band music. The singer was familiar with McDonald's group because she returned to Louisville regularly to perform at black theaters and also used some of the same musicians in her band. Martin and McDonald had another friend and band member in common as well: saxophonist Lucien Brown. Fiddler Henry Miles, who played with McDonald in the Ballard Chefs, told *Living Blues* in 1982, "We used to play with her [Martin]. Then I have a friend that used to play with her called Lucien Brown. See, they used to have a big theater here called the Lincoln Theatre, and she used to come here for shows. After she'd leave the shows, why, she'd come entertain somewhere else."

Victor Records agreed to the session with McDonald, Curtis Hayes, Clifford Hayes and Cal Smith because, earlier in 1924, a French label called Pathé had scored a few instrumental hits with quirky bands that featured novelty instruments like the kazoo, ukulele and comb. Victor was eager to cash in on the trend, so pairing Martin with a jug player seemed like a perfect opportunity. The Louisville Jug Band was already in New York at the time because of the Broadway producer who had arranged the trip after seeing the band play during a Kentucky Derby celebration. He helped the jug band book a stint at a club called the Garden of Joy.

"Jug Band Blues," a tune credited to McDonald and Hayes, is typical of the songs Martin recorded with their group. It is a mid-tempo blues tune about a woman who has been abandoned by her lover. Martin sang:

> *I woke up this morning, between midnight and day,*
> *you ought to see me hug the pillow, where my daddy used to lay*
> *I ain't got no daddy now, if my country goes to war*

I don't need no daddy no how
I'm singing this song for women like myself,
why you worry about a man, when you know he's got someone else?

Louisville jug music evolved from the string band tradition, but it is not folk music. The music McDonald and Hayes made is usually classified as early jazz because of Louisville's close association with New Orleans through riverboat commerce, as opposed to Memphis jug bands, which are more akin to the blues of the Mississippi Delta. The Louisville groups would later use jazz instruments like the saxophone, trumpet and piano on their records. But even in the traditional string band mode, as they were with Martin, these Louisville musicians could swing. McDonald, in particular, propels "Jug Band Blues" with a fluid, lilting bass line.

The jug musicians recorded ten songs with Martin over three sessions, including an instrumental version of "Jug Band Blues" and "Blue Devils Blues." The song "Papa Papa Blues" was credited to Clifford Hayes, McDonald and Martin. "I'm Gonna Be a Lovin's Old Soul" is attributed to only Martin and Clifford.

Victor issued the fruits of these sessions in 1925. These recordings gave the Louisville Jug Band the distinction of being the first jug band in the studio, but it beat Whistler's Jug Band by only about three days. Buford Threlkeld was known as Whistler because he played a nose whistle. Born in Eminence, Kentucky, in 1893, he moved to Louisville in 1914 and promptly founded a popular string band that featured B.D. Tite and, later, Rudolph "Jazz Lips" Thompson on jug.

In late September 1924, Whistler went into a studio in Richmond, Indiana, to record nine songs for Gennett Records. This included "In the Jailhouse," the minstrel show song that was also recorded by both Earl McDonald and Jimmie Rodgers. Although he would do other recording sessions for Gennett and, later, Okeh Records, Whistler did not have the long recording career of the McDonald- and Clifford Hayes–led groups. Part of this was from self-inflicted woes. Whistler apparently had a drug problem, and according to Cox, he left Louisville after being accused of stealing money from a guest's purse at a party.

This is sad because Whistler's Jug Band was a fine example of a black string band. There is incredible footage shot by ABC News in 1930 that shows the group on a farm performing the classic song "Foldin' Bed." The song is interesting because it features Whistler playing guitar along with three jug players. One of them is Thompson, who also performed with the Henry

Miles Jug Band and a number of other Louisville groups. Cox also believed that Whistler's Jug Band was the group mentioned in a 1920s newspaper article about a black jug band that performed at a Ku Klux Klan rally, but this has not been verified.

Earl McDonald and Clifford Hayes had greater success in the recording age than Whistler. They were back in the studio in November 1924 for Vocalion, making sides that would be issued under the Old Southern Jug Band. A humorous story occurred in 1926, when Ralph S. Peer sent a talent scout to Louisville to find McDonald and Hayes. A jug player named Henry Clifford convinced the record company that he was the Clifford of Clifford's Louisville Jug Band, one of the Louisville group's monikers. Henry then set out to hire McDonald and Hayes to play for him on the session. The ruse was soon straightened out. These sessions were ultimately released under the moniker of the Dixieland Jug Blowers, the most popular and influential of McDonald's groups. Cox points to this as a turning point in the Louisville jug band sound:

> *No previous jug band had ever dealt with the complexity of integrating a saxophone, a violin, three banjos, and two jugs into a working group…Few people, other than the musicians intimately associated with him, ever gave Earl McDonald due credit for his innate genius for getting the best musical performances possible out of any group and securing mutual co-operation to achieve a professional musical unity.*

The Dixieland Jug Blower sessions feature Dodds, who had played with similar groups back in New Orleans. The other musicians included Lockwood Lewis, a popular bandleader in his own right, on saxophone; Cal Smith on tenor banjo; Freddie Smith on plectrum banjo; Curtis Hayes on guitar and banjo; Clifford Hayes on fiddle; and two jug players, McDonald and Henry Clifford. These sessions were released by Victor Records and proved influential. This was the music Will Shade was referring to when he told Bengt Olsson, author of *Memphis Blues*, that the McDonald-Hayes recordings inspired him to start the seminal Memphis Jug Band.

In 1927, McDonald was back in the studio again for Columbia Records with Earl McDonald's Original Louisville Jug Band. Some of his best-known songs—"She's in the Graveyard Now," "Casey Bill" and "Under the Chicken Tree"—come from these sessions. The group was essentially the same as the Dixieland Jug Blowers. McDonald reteamed with Hayes under that moniker later in the year for more sessions for Victor. It would be one of their last together. From there on out, Hayes would focus on his jazz group, the Louisville Stompers, while McDonald turned to his more popular band, the Ballard Chefs.

The last known Hayes-McDonald recording session happened in 1931. Peer, the Victor chief, had a makeshift studio set up in a warehouse in downtown Louisville to record some white and black artists. This was the only postwar recording session to take place in Louisville. The main reason for the session was the collaboration between the label's two biggest hillbilly acts, Jimmie Rodgers and the Carter family.

Rodgers, known as the "Singing Brakeman," was born in Meridian, Mississippi, in 1897. He was first exposed to the music of African Americans when he worked on the railroad as a boy. He eventually left to work on a traveling show. Peer discovered Rodgers in 1927 in a famous Bristol, Tennessee session that was also the debut of the Carter Family, a musical dynasty that would later include June Carter Cash, wife of country singer Johnny Cash. The first generation of the Carter Family consisted of Alvin Pleasant "A.P." Carter; Sara Carter, his wife; and Maybelle Carter, who was married to A.P.'s brother Ezra (Eck) Carter and was also Sara's first cousin.

In an early form of corporate synergy, Peer wanted to advertise music with his two biggest groups on record together. However, the end result of the two acts together comes off as contrived and uninspired. Part of this is the setting. Although both tracks were recorded in Louisville, in one song, "T for Texas," the Carter Family pretends the group is visiting Rodgers in Kerriville, Texas. In the other song they recorded, Rodgers returns the favor and visits the Carter Family in West Virginia.

Other artists who recorded at the Louisville sessions were bluesmen Roosevelt Sykes, Walter Davis, Henry Townsend, Bill Gaither, J.D. Short and Louisville's Clifford Gibson, as well as two Louisville Jug Band–related artists: Kid Coley, who worked with Hayes, and Will "Bee" Ferguson, who is credited as Ben. Ferguson was backed by Earl McDonald's Original Louisville Jug Band on the recording date. According to Brenda Bogert, author of "The 1931 Louisville Victor Recording Session," the collaboration between Rodgers and the jug band was not planned. McDonald's group was working out a tune when Rodgers happened to walk by. Bogert wrote:

> *Apparently they were rehearsing the song "Please Don't Holler Mama" in the warehouse, when Jimmie Rodgers passed by and liked what he heard. Rodgers traveled with a briefcase filled with song lyrics written on sheets and scraps of paper. He could use these to "build" a song anytime he*

needed one. He would sometimes go so far as to make notes on his lyric sheets of the seemingly impromptu spoken comments that he would make during the song.

Rodgers's biographer, Barry Mazor, author of *Meeting Jimmie Rodgers*, says the singer was definitely acquainted with the Memphis Jug Band because of frequent visits to that city. And he mined the same musical territory as the Louisville Jug Band. As pointed out before, both acts recorded "In the Jailhouse Now," and they had an affinity for sampling blues, country and jazz. This was not the first Rodgers collaboration with a black artist. In 1930, he had recorded with trumpeter Louie Armstrong. Nolan Porterfield, author of *Jimmie Rodgers: The Life and Times of America's Blue Yodeler*, said of the Rodgers and McDonald group pairing:

The somewhat unusual instrumentation, not entirely representative of the true jug bands that worked the streets, is nevertheless singularly appropriate to the amalgamation of musical forms and traditions which found a form in the talents of Jimmie Rodgers: Clifford Hayes' bluesy country fiddle, the clean, single-string pick of Cal Smith on guitar (much of their work together reminds one of Django Reinhart and Stephane Grappelly), and the jazzy, moaning clarinet of George Allen, a brilliant if sometimes erratic musician.

The song they recorded, "My Good Gal's Gone Blues," is the same tune as "Try and Treat Her Right," one of the songs the jug band recorded that day with Ferguson. Rodgers seems to have worked the lyrics up right there in the studio. Rodgers seemed more comfortable with the jug band than he was with the Carter Family. During the song, he often calls out for McDonald to "blow that thing."

After this session, McDonald focused his attention on the Ballard Chefs. He was actually doing in-store appearances with a jug band promoting Ballard & Ballard Flour as early as 1928. The early version of the Ballard Chefs was basically Louisville Jug Band members: Cal Smith, Freddie Smith and Curtis Hayes. Henry Miles later joined on fiddle at the company's request. Ballard & Ballard sponsored a regional tour of the Ballard Chefs Jug Band that proved surprisingly popular and led to it investing more money in the group. Due to the support of the flour company, the Ballard Chefs began their own radio show in 1929 on WHAS in Louisville.

The show ended in 1932, but the group would still make a return to radio with a popular response from the listening public. On September

16, 1933, the *Chicago Defender* carried the headline: "Ballard's Jug Band Is Back on the Radio." The article reported that the radio show had made the Chefs a big draw in the Upper and Deep South. The group played for more than five thousand people in Raleigh, North Carolina, and the newspaper claimed that more than ten thousand tried to get into the auditorium. In 1934, the *Chicago Defender* reported that the Chefs were picked to represent Louisville in the "O, Sing a New Song" contest in Chicago. The group was sponsored by the *Louisville Defender*, which was an affiliate of the *Chicago Defender*, started in 1933. The Louisville paper, incidentally, was taken over by Frank Stanley Sr. in 1936. Among other things, Stanley wrote the report on the conditions of black troops that led the U.S. Army to desegregate after World War II.

In addition to the secular music, the Ballard Chefs backed up a gospel quartet. The October 5, 1930 edition of the *Louisville Leader* reads:

> *The Ballard Chefs, formerly the Smiley Brothers Quarette* [sic]*, featuring the Ballard Chefs' Jug Band packed the Hill Street Baptist Church Tuesday night in their Grand Musical Recital presentation which included spiritual, jubilee, popular songs, comedy, and plantation numbers by the quartette and jug band and solos by Mrs. Rebecca Lee which also thrilled the crowd composed of white and colored friends of the Ballard Chefs who are heard every Monday night over WHAS for*

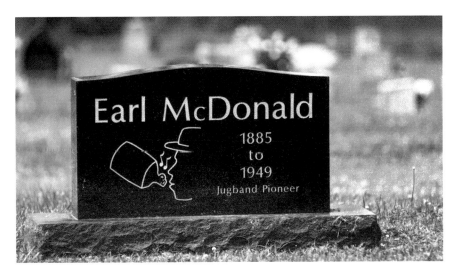

Jug blower Earl McDonald's grave site in Louisville Cemetery. The gravestone was purchased by the National Jug Band Jubilee in 2009. *Photo by Brian Bohannon.*

the Ballard and Ballard Company. Miss Kathleen Beason who is at the piano for the chef's on Monday nights also served for Mrs. Lee, who is easily one of Louisville's leading sopranos.

The Ballard Chefs continued to be a popular live act even after the WHAS show ended in 1932. McDonald led the group until the early 1940s, but he also had to work as a porter at Shackleton Piano Company. That was his main occupation when he died in 1949. He was buried in an unmarked grave in the Louisville Cemetery. The civil rights generation looked on jug music as a sad product of a bygone era, and Earl's success was soon forgotten by all but a faithful few fans. Miles continued the Ballard Chefs under the banner the Henry Miles Jug Band until 1966. There was some interest in McDonald's work during the 1960s folk revival, but the jug player wouldn't get the recognition he deserved until the National Jug Band Jubilee was founded in 2005. Three years later, the organizers of the festival would raise $1,200 to buy McDonald a tombstone.

Chapter 6

The Juggernaut Jug Band and the Folk Revival

We do versions of 'Black Dog,' 'Pinball Wizard' and 'You Really Got Me.'
That's in keeping with the original jug musicians, who would use kazoos to play
'Cocktail for Two' or whatever else they heard on the radio. I guess there will
always be a market for novelty music.
— Steve "the Amazing Mr. Gil Fish" Drury, leader of the Juggernaut Jug Band

Henry Miles was born in Samuels, Kentucky, in 1905. He moved to Louisville around 1922. Miles played in children's street bands before joining the Mike Perkins Jug Band in 1926. Three years later, he quit that group to play with Earl McDonald in the Ballard Chefs. After McDonald's death in 1949, the fiddler took over the band and renamed it the Henry Miles Jug Band. The group featured jug player Rudolph "Jazz Lips" Thompson, who had played with Whistler's Jug Band and the Mud Gutter Jug Band. Blues singer John "Preacher" Stephens also played spoons with the group.

For many years, the Henry Miles Jug Band was the only connection Louisville had to its jug band tradition. The group continued to play around town throughout the 1950s. It even performed at the 1965 World's Fair in New York City. But Miles went into semi-retirement from music after Thompson died in 1966. To his last day, the fiddler was convinced that McDonald and Thompson had passed before their time due to the hazards of jug blowing.

"Since I've been playing, I lost 18 men," he told *Living Blues* in 1982. "I lost my last jug player in 1966. Rudolph Thompson. He was A-No. 1. And

Earl McDonald was A-No. 1. There wasn't but two. Of course, there's a lot of others that blowed jugs but they couldn't come up to them. They were kings. And I've never been able to get another jug player. See, it was a strain on 'em when they played. So you don't hear 'em now."

One day in the late 1960s, a young, white jug player showed up at Miles's door. Everyone knows Ralph S. Helm as Roscoe Goose, the stage name he adopted as member of the Juggernaut Jug Band, a group founded in 1965 by his older brother, Steve Helm, and some high school friends. The Juggernauts were a product of the folk revival, and Roscoe was seeking some connection to earlier generations of jug musicians. In early 2013, Roscoe sat in the kitchen of his mother's house and talked about the time he spent at Miles's home on Chestnut Street.

"I was talking to Vy Synder at the musicians' union about

The Henry Miles Jug Band featuring jug player Rudolph Thompson. Miles took over the Ballard Chefs after Earl McDonald died and he renamed the group. *Courtesy of the University of Louisville Photographic Archives & Special Collections.*

wanting to talk to someone from the old jug band community," Roscoe remembered. "She found Henry for me. Henry was the most gracious, kindest, warmest fellow unless you asked him to come play with white boys. That wasn't going to happen. He didn't care about playing much of anything when I was sitting with him in his living room. This was not a jam session. He just talked."

Miles told him stories about guys he knew. How Earl McDonald liked to sing dirty songs. He talked about the guys Clifford Hayes had beat out of money. Mostly, they talked about music. Miles told Roscoe about a tune called "Airplane" that all the old jug bands did. Roscoe has never been able to figure out what song the older musician was talking about, and he's been searching for forty years.

One day, Roscoe asked, "Henry, what is a jug band?"

Miles thought about it for a minute, and then he answered, "You can have a symphony orchestra. If you got a jug player in that band, that's a jug band." Roscoe has used that answer as a defense through the years when people have questioned whether the Juggernaut Jug Band is a true jug band because it sometimes does original songs and rock covers like "People Are Strange."

"I always say we are a jug band because we got the jug," Roscoe explained.

> That's just like Henry Miles said. I've never cared as much if we had a big connection to the old jug bands. I'm a big fan of what they did. I think it's a great genre, a great repertoire of what record collectors called prewar blues. Really, it's the roots of the blues. The Louisville jug band recordings reflect a real attempt to be jazz, hard swinging jazzy bands. The Juggernaut Jug Band is its own thing. We are not trying to be the same as the old jug bands.

The Juggernaut Jug Band discovered jug music by listening to albums by Jim Kweskin's Jug Band and Dave Von Ronk. For many years, they were ignorant of the fact that the genre originated in their own hometown. Jug band music went into a steep decline in popularity during the Depression, and young people had almost no interest in it by the 1950s, when the first strains of rock-and-roll were hitting the airwaves.

At the time, American folk and early blues was still popular in England. In 1956, Lonnie Donegan had a British hit with a cover of Leadbelly's "Rock Island Line." That song helped ignite the Skiffle music craze, which saw young musicians playing American folk and jug band songs on found or homemade instruments like tea chests, cigar box guitars

Roscoe Goose of the Juggernaut Jug Band at the 2009 Jubilee. Roscoe is the only currently active jug player in Louisville. *Photo by O'Neil Arnold, courtesy of the National Jug Band Jubilee.*

and washboards. Jimmy Page, the Hollies and the Beatles all started out playing in Skiffle bands.

American teenagers rediscovered their own country's early folk culture in the 1960s. Bands like Kweskin's Jug Band and Mother McCree's Uptown Jug Champions, a group led by Jerry Garcia of the Grateful Dead, started to look backward for the real America. Jim Kweskin's Jug Band was one of the best versed of the new generation of these mostly white bands. The group recorded "Overseas Stomp," a Clifford Hayes tune about Charles Lindbergh's flight over the Atlantic Ocean.

John Jacob Niles was a direct link between Louisville and the American folk revival that was centered in New York's Greenwich Village. Niles was born in 1892 in Louisville, where he was exposed to vaudeville shows and jug band music. After serving in World War I, he studied music in France and at the Cincinnati Conservatory of Music. In 1925, Niles moved to New York City, where he came into contact with early folk artists like Joan Baez,

Burl Ives and Peter, Paul and Mary. Niles transcribed traditional songs like "Pretty Polly" and "He's Goin' Away," and he wrote his own originals. "Go 'Way from My Window" is probably his most popular tune. He eventually retired to Clark County, Kentucky, where he lived on Boot Hill Farm until he died in 1980.

Roscoe's brother Steve Helm and his friend John Fish were two of the kids listening to the work Niles and the new folk bands were putting out. In 1965, inspired by these traditional sounds, they decided to start their own group with John on banjo-ukulele and Steve on guitar. They also recruited guitarist Don Oswald, Fred Glock on jug and Roscoe on washboard and harmonica. John had a little more time than the others to devote to the band because he had already graduated high school the year before. He searched through the dictionary for a name when he came across the word juggernaut, which in Hinduism is an incarnation of the god Krishna, depicted as a wheel. It was also an unstoppable force.

"That first incarnation of the band was a lot of fun and dear to everyone's heart," Roscoe said. "We learned a lot of Kweskin material. I don't think it lasted past the summer. People went off to college and different things."

Oswald and Roscoe tried to keep the band going after the others had moved on. In 1968, the Juggernaut Jug Band performed at Waggener High School's vaudeville show, with its friend Steve Drury on a washtub bass and Oswald on guitar. With Glock gone, Roscoe took over jug duties, which he would handle for the next four decades. Jug playing is more about the player than the container. "The jug is just an amplifier, a resonating chamber for sound," Roscoe said. Pointing at his lips, he added, "The sound comes from here. You've got to blow straight into it and have a good sense of pitch and know what you are going after. It is like anything else; it doesn't just happen."

This second incarnation of the Juggernaut Jug Band didn't last long either. Pretty soon, Roscoe was off to the navy, and Drury and Oswald were headed to college. However, when Roscoe returned in 1973, he found his friends ready to get serious about the band. Inspired by the Star-Spangled Washboard Band from Albany, New York, the Juggernauts decided they needed to be more theatrical. The washboard band played great music, but it also put on a show. That group had colorful stage names, so the Juggernaut Jug Band members decided to get some new names, too. Oswald became Dr. Don almost immediately, and it didn't take long for Ralph S. Helm to become Roscoe Goose. The name comes from a Louisville-born jockey who won the 1913 Kentucky Derby and a multitude of other races.

Fred Glock at a jug workshop. Glock is a frequent volunteer at the National Jug Band Jubilee. *Photo by Brian Bohannon, courtesy of National Jug Band Jubilee.*

The Juggernaut Jug Band was driving to a show at the Jefferson Davis Inn in Lexington, Kentucky, when they happened to see a plaque dedicated to the jockey. "Don says, 'That's you,'" Roscoe remembered. "The name kind of stuck ever since. That same night, [Steve Drury] was playing, and he had a rubber fish in his pocket. The tail was sticking out of his pocket. Someone in the audience spied that fish tail waggin' in his pocket. They started yellin', 'Hey, Mr. Fish.' That was it. He was the Amazing Mr. Gil Fish."

The reformed Juggernauts also included Carrol "Easy Mark" Ohlson, who, along with Dr. Don, began writing original material for the band. Their set would feature these songs, along with standards like the Memphis Jug Band's "Jug Band Music" and a few rock covers. The group was good enough to get a manager, Tom Sobel, and a gig at the Butchertown Pub every Friday for four years. There were always questions about their authenticity, but to this day, Roscoe Goose is the only working jug player in Louisville.

Still, Steve Drury's wife, Alison, remembers some especially non–jug band moments through the years. "The first time I saw the Juggernauts, I went with Fish to a practice in the Helm basement," she said. "They had an agent that lived in Cincinnati. He wanted to book them as a jug band, but he also

Old Southern Jug Blowers, a Japanese jug band, on stage with Juggernaut Jug Band members Steve "Mr. Fish" Drury (bass) and Roscoe Goose, 2009 Jubilee. *Photo by O'Neil Arnold, courtesy of the National Jug Band Jubilee.*

wanted them do something else in the same city. They could do a listening room here and then do a disco. They actually had a disco act. It was awful. It was a very short period of time."

Roscoe dropped out of the Juggernaut Jug Band in the early '80s and spent his time working in a warehouse for a construction company. He stayed away from jug band music for fourteen years, but he did have a blues group called "Roscoe Goose and the Honkers" in the late '80s. Drury kept the Juggernaut Jug Band going without him for nearly a decade, but things started to slow down in the early 1990s. The group probably would have ended again if Roscoe hadn't gotten a call from Sobel. Their old manager had opened a comedy club, the Comedy Caravan, in the Highlands neighborhood in Louisville. He wanted to know if Roscoe would like to get a band together to perform on Wednesday nights. Sobel offered the group thirty dollars a night and free drinks to play. It wasn't much, but Roscoe was itching to pick up the jug again. He called Drury, who was operating the Hitching Post Saddle Shop in Middletown with his wife. They took the gig.

This version of the Juggernaut Jug Band kept going until it was as much an institution as some of Earl McDonald's old bands. In a few years, the group became a full-time job for everyone involved. In addition to the live shows, it also began recording albums. The band's first release, *Perhaps You Don't Recognize Us*, featured classic tunes like "Chicken Tree" and a cover of "Black Dog." It took them a few decades, but they finally fulfilled all the dreams the Juggernauts had when Roscoe got out of the navy in 1973.

Other musicians came and went through the years, but Mr. Fish and Roscoe Goose remained constants in the band for most of its existence. For many years, the Juggernaut Jug Band had a monthly gig at Clifton Pizza on Frankfort Avenue in Louisville. The group also traveled to over twenty-five states and Canada performing and giving talks about jug band music. The Juggernauts even created a special outreach program for schools. In 2009, the Louisville Metro Council named them "Ambassadors of Goodwill." This was also the year Mr. Fish died. Roscoe continued the Juggernauts with a new crop of musicians. He said the group is not the same without his old friend, but the Juggernauts must keep rolling along.

"There have been a lot of versions of this jug band," Roscoe declared. "The one thing they all have in common is that they've all been fun. That's why we are the Juggernaut Jug Band. We are unstoppable—kinda like jug band music itself."

Mark Blackwell of the Lost Shoe String Band blowing some jug at the 2010 National Jug Band Jubilee. *Photo by Brian Bohannon, courtesy of the National Jug Band Jubilee.*

Above: Jack Pignatello (Hawaiian shirt) and Mark Blackwell (brown vest) blowing jug at the 2009 National Jug Band Jubilee. *Photo by O'Neil Arnold, courtesy of the National Jug Band Jubilee.*

Left: This instrument belongs to Gnarly Snag of the Smokin' Fez Monkeys. *Photo by O'Neil Arnold, courtesy of the National Jug Band Jubilee.*

And this *is* Gnarly Snag of the Smokin' Fez Monkeys. *Photo by O'Neil Arnold, courtesy of the National Jug Band Jubilee.*

From left to right: Roscoe Goose of the Juggernaut Jug Band, a member of the Old Southern Jug Blowers and Fred Glock, former member of the Juggernaut Jug Band. *Photo by O'Neil Arnold, courtesy of the National Jug Band Jubilee.*

Left: Dwight "Blind Boy Chocolate" Hawkins playing some saw. He also performs occasionally with the Crow Quill Night Owls. *Photo by Brian Bohannon, courtesy of National Jug Band Jubilee.*

Below, from left to right: Roscoe Goose of the Juggernaut Jug Band, two members of the Old Southern Jug Blowers and Fred Glock, former member of the Juggernaut Jug Band. *Photo by O'Neil Arnold, courtesy of National Jug Band Jubilee.*

Attendees of the National Jug Band Jubilee practice the saw under the watchful eye of Dwight "Blind Boy Chocolate" Hawkins. *Photo by Brian Bohannon, courtesy of National Jug Band Jubilee.*

The Hokum High Rollers of New Orleans at the 2013 National Jug Band Jubilee. The group specializes in pre–World War II Piedmont blues, ragtime, hot jazz and western swing played with the grit of their hometown and the energy of their punk rock roots. *Photo by Brian Bohannon, courtesy of National Jug Band Jubilee.*

The Blair Street Mugwumps from Portland, Oregon, at the 2010 National Jug Band Jubilee. Jug band music is popular with young musicians in the Pacific Northwest. *Photo by Brian Bohannon, courtesy of National Jug Band Jubilee.*

Learning how to blow the jug during a jug band workshop. *Photo by Brian Bohannon, courtesy of National Jug Band Jubilee.*

Eric "Hambone" Buhrer of the Cincinnati Dancing Pigs teaching a jug-blowing workshop. The group is a fixture at the National Jug Band Jubilee. *Photo by Brian Bohannon, courtesy of National Jug Band Jubilee.*

Kit Stymee Stovepipe of the Crow Quill Night Owls at the 2013 National Jug Band Jubilee. The group is among the most popular of the new generation of jug bands. Kit also plays in folk-blues singer Maria Muldaur's backing band. *Photo by Brian Bohannon, courtesy of National Jug Band Jubilee.*

Arlo Leach of the How Long Jug Band, Portland, Oregon. Leach helped establish the Jug Band Hall of Fame. *Photo by Brian Bohannon, courtesy of National Jug Band Jubilee.*

Above: National Jug Band Jubilee president Heather Leoncini and her mother, Alison Drury, widow of Steve "Mr. Fish" Drury. Leoncini has led the Jubilee since its founders died. *Photo by Brian Bohannon, courtesy of the National Jug Band Jubilee.*

Left: Giued Lutge of the How Long Jug Band, Portland, Oregon, at the 2013 National Jug Band Jubilee. They are another popular group from the Pacific Northwest. *Photo by Brian Bohannon, courtesy of National Jug Band Jubilee.*

Washboard—mysterious fingers! There are no washboards on the early Louisville jug band recordings although it was used by some street bands. *Photo by Brian Bohannon, courtesy of National Jug Band Jubilee.*

Aaron Baer and Jeff Mitchell of the Jackson Street Polecats, Oshkosh, Wisconsin, at the 2012 National Jug Band Jubilee. *Photo by Brian Bohannon, courtesy of National Jug Band Jubilee.*

Above: Rob Davis of the Roe Family Singers at the 2010 National Jug Band Jubilee. *Photo by Brian Bohannon, courtesy of National Jug Band Jubilee.*

Left: Y'uns Jug Band at the 2010 National Jug Band Jubilee. J.P. Reddick on guitar/vocal/kazoo/siren. *Photo by Brian Bohannon, courtesy of National Jug Band Jubilee.*

Chapter 7
The National Jug Band Jubilee

They talked to me about [how] *they're going to have a big thing, sometime this year in October, and try to get my dad into the musical hall of fame for Kentucky. And that's something. It's just, I don't know what to think about that.*
—Mattie Mathis, Earl McDonald's daughter

The first time Rod Wenz heard jug music was at the 2002 Birmingham City Stages, an arts and music festival in Birmingham, Alabama. Wenz was a retired public relations executive who spent most of his free time indulging a newfound interest in folk music and early jazz. He and his wife, Gloria Wenz, traveled to festivals all over the country in search of good tunes. The couple was actually heading to an exit when Rod heard some music that sounded familiar yet strange to him. He recognized elements of Dixieland jazz in it, but there were also hints of blues and even bluegrass. What really caught his attention was the guy playing the bass parts by blowing into a jug.

Despite the fact that it was raining lightly, Rod asked his wife if she minded sitting and listening for a minute. She agreed, and they found a spot near the stage. The couple ended up staying for the entire set by the Juggernaut Jug Band. When the show was over, Rod saw the group's leader, Steve "the Amazing Mr. Gil Fish" Drury, heading to his car with some equipment. They followed him.

Rod asked, "What do you call that music you guys play?"

"Jug band music."

"Oh," Rod said. "I never heard of it."

Gloria asked, "Where are you guys from?"

Rod Wenz in office of National Jug Band Jubilee headquarters, his house! Wenz founded the festival in 2005 with Steve Drury of the Juggernaut Jug Band. *Courtesy of the National Jug Band Jubilee.*

Drury answered, "It's a town you probably never heard of—Louisville, Kentucky."

Gloria slapped him lightly on the shoulder. "You've got to be kidding," she said with a giggle.

Drury was confused. "Why kidding?"

"Because that's where we're from," she said.

For years, it would bother Rod that he had to go all the way to Alabama to find out about music that was born in his adopted hometown. Rod, born on December 21, 1935, was originally from North Platte, Nebraska. He started writing for the *North Platte Telegraph-Bulletin* while he was still in high school. After attending the University of Nebraska, Rod became city editor at the *Fremont Guide and Tribune*. In 1959, he moved to Illinois to cover local government for the *Rockford Register-Republic*. He wrote a series of articles on the conditions at Illinois' largest institution for the mentally retarded that won an award from the American Political Science Association and was entered in the competition for a Pulitzer Prize.

Rod was working as a public relations representative for Chrysler Corporation in Belvidere, Illinois, in 1967, when he got an opportunity to move to Kentucky.

He joined the *Louisville Courier-Journal* as a reporter but soon became the paper's city editor. In 1971, he left journalism for the public relations business. Rod and Randy Neely formed the firm Wenz-Neely, which they ran for eighteen years until they sold it to a British company. After his retirement, Rod immersed himself in music.

Rod got in touch with Drury not long after he and Gloria returned from Alabama. The men were quick friends. Rod and his wife became regulars at the Juggernaut Jug Band's monthly performances at Clifton's Pizza. Each month, they took a different couple with them to see the Juggernauts. Rod wanted everyone to know about this great thing he had discovered. The more he heard jug music, the more he liked it. Rod began researching the history of the genre in his spare time. He couldn't understand why jug band music wasn't as celebrated in Louisville as the blues in Memphis or jazz in New Orleans.

Drury became his tutor, turning him on to music and talking to him about the history of jug playing, but he also had a secret agenda. He knew that Rod had a lot of contacts from his days in business. One day, Drury suggested Rod use these contacts to help promote jug music somehow. Maybe put on a show. Gloria Wenz remembers that Rod was reluctant to take on the project at first. "He said, 'I can write, but I don't know any bands,'" Gloria remembered. "Every excuse he made, Fish would have an answer. He said, 'I know the bands. I'll take care of that. You just put it together.' That's when they decided to do the first Jubilee."

Drury traveled a lot with the Juggernaut Jug Band, but he gave Rod some days when the band was available. Rod found out that the *Belle of Louisville*, the last Mississippi River steamboat still in operation, was looking for someone to put on a music event. The operators of the boat thought a jug band cruise was a good idea, but they wanted two bands. Drury recruited the Cincinnati Dancing Pigs. It was decided that a cruise would be a perfect way to test the interest for a jug band music festival.

"We had six weeks to publicize what we were doing," Gloria said. "Rod knew a lot of businesspeople, so he went to them and told them that they should buy a table of eight for fifty dollars a person. They did. I'm not bragging about this, but Rod did a lot of stuff for people. He was on the mayor's committee for the airport. He called in every favor he could. We got two hundred people."

After they had invited all of these guests, Rod and Gloria learned that the *Belle* didn't provide food. The members of Louisville Originals, an organization of local restaurants, agreed to provide food, but they couldn't deliver it. Drury's daughter, Heather Leoncini, helped him with Juggernaut Jug Band business, so he volunteered her to organize the shuttling of the food to the boat. She would be the festival's official jack-of-all-trades for years to come and, later, its president.

A stylish washboard, courtesy of the National Jug Band Jubilee. *Photo by Brian Bohannon, courtesy of National Jug Band Jubilee.*

What Rod and Drury didn't count on was the fact that tourists staying at the downtown Louisville hotels would also be interested in what was happening on the *Belle*. He let in anyone who would pay the fifty-dollar admission. Instead of the two hundred people he was prepared for, the first edition of what became the National Jug Band Jubilee had four hundred people.

"We ran out of food," Gloria admitted. "We were so embarrassed, but the *Belle* made a fortune because they did the liquor. Afterward, they would ask us if we wanted to do it again. We said if we did, we'd get the liquor, too. But that's how it got started. Almost as soon as the first one was over, people were asking when we were going to do it again."

The cruise took place on July 1, 2005. Rod knew immediately that he had something. He registered the National Jug Band Jubilee as a nonprofit. At first, he was financing the Jubilee with his own money. But he started putting together a board of directors to raise money from corporate donors. Drury's wife, Alison, quipped, "If you talked to Rod once you were on the Jubilee board. I think every businessperson in the city might have been listed at one time or another."

It took a while for Rod to find a permanent home for his festival. The Jubilee took place on the campus of St. Joseph's Children's Home in 2006. It was at the Iroquois Amphitheater in 2007. But in 2008, the National Jug Band Jubilee made an agreement with the Louisville Waterfront Development Corporation to use the Brown-Forman Amphitheater on the third Saturday in September each year. That was the first year the festival was free to the public. What started out as a short cruise on the *Belle of Louisville* is now a family-friendly, all-day festival that attracts thousands of people to see bands from all over the country. The festival has introduced jug band fans to new groups like the Grammy award–winning Carolina Chocolate Drops, who played the festival twice in the early years, and the Crow Quill Night Owls, a popular West Coast group.

"Jug band music is called river music, and now we're on the river," said Leoncini, who became president after Rod died in November 2008. "We love it. Every year, we are attracting more people. There is a huge contingent that comes from out of town for this—as far as California, New Jersey and New York."

An important early benefactor of the Jubilee was Sara Elizabeth Shallenberger "Sally" Brown, the matriarch of one of Louisville's wealthiest families and one of the city's leading philanthropists. Brown was a friend and longtime patron of Earl McDonald, who often played private parties hosted by her late husband, W.L. Lyons Brown Sr., chairman and president of distiller Brown-Forman Corp., which was founded by his grandfather. Sally Brown died in May 2011, a month after she celebrated her 100th birthday. She gave generously to the Jubilee in her later years, and when her health was too fragile for her to attend the festival in person, the organization showed its appreciation by sending a jug band to entertain her at home.

"Mrs. Brown had four really favorite jug band songs," Jubilee board member David Wood told the *Louisville Courier-Journal* after Brown's death.

She loved a song called "Tear It Down." She'd always tap her toe and smile. Another one was "Eve Wasn't Modest Til She Ate That Apple," she liked "Under the Chicken Tree," and the fourth song is called "Beans." In fact, my first exposure to jug band music was in the mid-'50s when Mrs. Brown and her family had a party and the entertainment was the Henry Miles Jug Band. She helped underwrite the concerts, was very instrumental in getting it on the waterfront, and when she was older and not physically able to attend, we would get a jug band, pile them into a van and give her a 45-minute concert right there in her home. She'd be thrilled.

There was a dedication ceremony for Brown at the 2011 Jubilee. Wood and David Karem, president of the Louisville Waterfront Development Corporation, which operates Waterfront Park, spoke about her love of jug band music. One of the songs she liked, "Tear It Down," is a variation of the classic tune "Foldin' Bed," which was recorded by Whistler's Jug Band. In the 1930s, Basil Duke Henning from Louisville took "Tear It Down" to Yale University, where it became a standard song performed by the famous a cappella Yale singing group, the Whiffenpoofs, for many years.

Over the years, the Jubilee developed a reputation among folk musicians. When Rod was alive, he was getting band submissions from as far away as Japan and Australia. The Old Southern Jug Blowers, a group of Japanese musicians enamored of Earl McDonald's music, were the most persistent. They loved McDonald so much that they learned his songs phonetically, even though most of them didn't speak English. The group had been playing Louisville jug music for Japanese audiences for years when they learned about the National Jug Band Jubilee.

The Old Southern Jug Blowers contacted Rod, who told them that the festival could not afford to bring them to America. If they paid their own passage, the Jubilee could put them up and find them other shows to make the trip worth the musicians' time. The band held fundraisers in Japan for a couple of years before they could take the trip. Finally, in 2009, the Old Southern Jug Blowers made it to Louisville. They actually performed at McDonald's grave when his new tombstone, purchased with money raised through the Jubilee, was unveiled. Before he died, Rod also tried unsuccessfully to have McDonald enshrined in the Kentucky Music Hall of Fame. He was able to get a plaque dedicated to the jug player placed in Waterfront Park.

Drury passed away in November 2009. Since then, Leoncini has operated the festival with a board of volunteers. "After Rod passed, Gloria, his widow, said straight up, 'We have to keep this going,'" Leoncini exclaimed. "Of course, my dad and I agreed. He got more involved and helped me keep the next year's event going. Honestly, when my dad passed away, it was not even an option not to keep going."

The 2010 National Jug Band Jubilee was a tribute to Jubilee founders, Rod Wenz and Steve Drury. It also included the first inductions to the Jug Band Hall of Fame, which is currently only an online resource (www.jughall.org) but the Jubilee board hopes to find it a permanent, physical home in upcoming years. Among the first inductees in the Hall of Fame was jug player Earl McDonald. His granddaughter Terri Brown was there to accept the honor. McDonald's daughter, Mattie Mathis, only attended one Jubilee, 2006, before she passed in October 2010 at the age of seventy-eight.

Leoncini is pleased to be part of a jug music family and to be playing a role in passing on the genre to future generations in Louisville. "One of my favorite things is when we do the workshops at the Jubilee and little kids come up and learn how to play," she said. "I always smile when I see little kids playing washboards and jugs. That signifies to me that the music is going to keep going on."

Afterword

Nothing drove home the current state of jug band music in popular culture better than a talk I had with Terri Brown, Earl McDonald's granddaughter. I was pumping her for information about the jug player, and she finally admitted, "You know more about my grandfather than I do." Nothing else better illustrates the disconnection between the jug band generation and the modern world. This is unfortunate because jug music still has a lot to offer contemporary music fans.

Jug music is an obscure musical intersection where the blues, country music, bluegrass and jazz come together. In understanding why these genres went their separate ways, we also learn something about American character. People in the United States tend to ignore history that does not make them feel better, but in avoiding the past, they also throw away some of the things that make this country unique and interesting. Jug music is a hybrid of European melodies and African rhythms that was forged during one of the most divisive times in our history. But it also represents a space where slaves and masters, black and white people, the rich and the poor, came together to enjoy themselves.

African Americans abandoned string band music after the 1930s because it did not speak to their aspirations for the future. But Earl McDonald and his generation had the same dreams and hopes for their own kids. They put all their souls into forging a new sound that is part of our blood memory even if we don't acknowledge it. Dwight Hawkins, one of the few black neo-string band musicians, teaches a class at the National Jug Band Jubilee under the moniker "Saw Man." One day, I asked him how to play the jug, and he said that if you can beatbox, you can play the jug. There has never been any research to positively connect jug playing to beatboxing in hip-hop, but it is not far-fetched to assume that the practices are linked by black culture.

This study is aimed at general fans of American folk music, but I also hope that it helps other African Americans to appreciate the genre as being representative of our common American legacy. There is something enduring about jug band music that has carried it from the nineteenth to the twenty-first century. That's because the practice of jug blowing continues to inspire and entertain audiences of all ages, races and social statuses. This is good-time music, and everybody deserves to dance.

Bibliography

BOOKS

Conway, Cecelia. *African Banjo Echoes in Appalachia: A Study of Folk Traditions.* Knoxville: University of Tennessee Press, 1999.

Cox, Fred. "The Jug Bands of Louisville." Unpublished ms., excerpted in *Storyville Magazine* (1995): 156–61.

Davis, Francis. *The History of the Blues: The Roots, the Music, the People, from Charley Patton to Robert Cray.* New York: Mojo Working Productions, 1995.

Durrett, Reuben Thomas. *The Romance of the Origin of Louisville.* Louisville, KY, 1894.

Epstein, Dena P. *Sinful Tunes and Spirituals: Black Folk Music to the Civil War.* Urbana: University of Illinois Press, 1981.

Gibson, Williams. *History of the United Brothers of Friendship and Sisters of the Mysterious Ten, a Negro Order Organized August 1, 1861 in the City of Louisville, Ky. Containing Photos, Sketches, and Narratives of the Lives of Its Founders and Organizers.* Louisville, KY, 1861.

Gioia, Ted. *The History of Jazz.* New York: Oxford University Press, 1997.

Harrison, Daphne Duval. *Black Pearls: Blues Queens of the 1920s.* New Brunswick, NJ: Rutgers University Press, 1988.

Herskovits, Melville J. *The Myth of the Negro Past.* Boston: Beacon Press, 1958.

Keil, Charles. *Urban Blues.* Chicago: University of Chicago Press, 1991.

Levine, Lawrence. *Black Culture and Black Consciousness: African American Thought from Freedom to Slavery.* London: Oxford University Press, 2007.

Mazor, Barry. *Meeting Jimmie Rodgers*. New York: Oxford University Press, 2009.

Oliver, Paul. *Songsters & Saints*. New York: Cambridge University Press, 1984.

Olsson, Bengt. *Memphis Blues*. London: Studio Vista, 1970.

Packet, Mary. *Steamboatin' Days: Folk Songs of the River Packet Era*. Baton Rouge: Louisiana State University Press, 1944.

Palmer, Robert. *Deep Blues*. New York: Penguin Books, 1981.

Pecknold, Diana, ed. *Hidden in the Mix: The African American Presence in Country Music*. Durham, NC: Duke University Press, 2013.

Pen, Ron. *I Wonder as I Wander: The Life of John Jacob Niles*. Lexington: University Press of Kentucky, 2010.

Peretti, Burton. *The Creation of Jazz: Music, Race, and Culture in Urban America*. Urbana: University of Illinois Press, 1994.

Porterfield, Nolan. *Jimmie Rodgers: The Life and Times of America's Blue Yodeler*. Urbana: University of Illinois Press, 1979.

Sterns, Marshall. *The Story of Jazz*. New York: Oxford University Press, 1958.

Toll, Robert. *Blacking Up: The Minstrel Show in Nineteenth Century America*. New York: Oxford University Press, 1974.

Wright, George. *Life Behind a Veil: Blacks in Louisville, Kentucky, 1865–1930*. Baton Rouge: Louisiana State University Press, 1985.

ARTICLES

Baptist, Edward E. "Cuffy, Fancy Maids, and One-Eyed Men: Rape, Commodification, and the Domestic Slave Trade in the United States." *American Historical Review* 106, no. 5 (December 2001): 1619–50.

Blackwood, B.M., and Henry Balfour. "Ritual and Secular Uses of Vibrating Membranes as Voice-Disguisers." *Journal of the Royal Anthropological Institute of Great Britain and Ireland* 78, no. 1/2 (1948): 45–69.

Bogert, Brenda. "The 1931 Louisville Victor Recording Session." *Blues News*, 1993.

Brauneis, Robert. "Copyright and the World's Most Popular Song." *Journal of the Copyright Society of the U.S.A.* 335 (2009), George Washington University Legal Studies Research Paper No. 392.

Flemons, Dom. "Can You Blame Gus Cannon?" *Oxford American*, 2014, 83.

"Henry Miles and the Louisville Jug Bands." *Living Blues*, 1982, 51.

Livers, Bill. Interview by Burnham Ware. *Living Blues*, 1982, 51.

About the Author

Michael L. Jones is an award-winning journalist who resides in Louisville, Kentucky. He is the author of *Second-Hand Stories: 15 Portraits of Louisville* (Weeping Buddha Press). He also sits on the board of directors of the National Jug Band Jubilee, a nationally renowned festival that celebrates a form of pre–World War II folk music that originated in Louisville. Jones has been a staff writer for the *Louisville Courier-Journal*, the *Louisville Eccentric Observer* (*LEO*), the *Jeffersonville Evening News* and the *Louisville Defender*. He is married with three stepchildren.

Visit us at
www.historypress.net

··

This title is also available as an e-book